Flight

Teacher's Guide

Read Well 1 • Unit 38

igh

igh says /igh/.
Continuous Sound
Voiced (Long)

o_e

/o_e/
Bossy E
Voiced (Long)

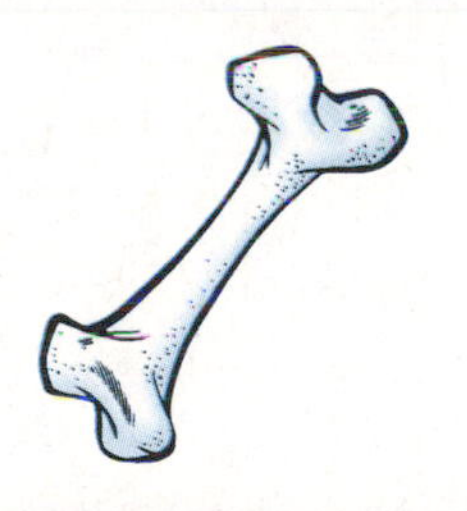

ir

ir says /ir/.
Voiced
R-Controlled

Critical Foundations in Primary Reading

Marilyn Sprick, Lisa Howard, Ann Fidanque, Shelley V. Jones

ISBN 13-digit: 978-1-59318-461-2 ISBN 10-digit: 1-59318-461-1 132100/2-12

11 12 13 RRDHRBVA 15 14 13 12

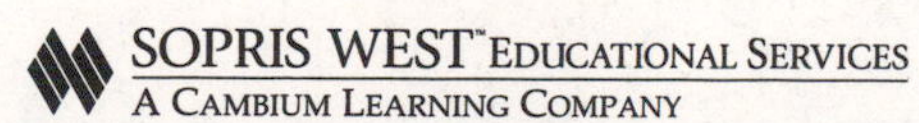
SOPRIS WEST™ EDUCATIONAL SERVICES
A CAMBIUM LEARNING COMPANY

BOSTON, MA • LONGMONT, CO

Table of Contents

Unit 38

Flight

How to Teach the Lessons

How to Teach the Lessons (*continued*)

End of the Unit

Read Well I Sequence and Sound Pronunciation Guide

I /I/ **I** Voiced (Word) **Unit A**	Mm /mmm/ **Monkey** Continuous Voiced **Unit B**	Ss /sss/ **Snake** Continuous Unvoiced **Unit 1**	Ee /eee/ **Emu** Continuous Voiced (Long) **Unit 2**	ee /eeee/ **Bee** Continuous Voiced (Long) **Unit 2**	Mm /mmm/ **Monkey** Continuous Voiced **Unit 3**
Aa /aaa/ **Ant** Continuous Voiced (Short) **Unit 4**	Dd /d/ **Dinosaur** Quick Voiced (not duh) **Unit 5**	th /ththth/ **the** Continuous Voiced **Unit 6**	Nn /nnn/ **Nest** Continuous Voiced **Unit 7**	Tt /t/ **Turkey** Quick Unvoiced (not tuh) **Unit 8**	Ww /www/ **Wind** Continuous Voiced (woo) **Unit 9**
Ii /iii/ **Insects** Continuous Voiced (Short) **Unit 10**	Th /Ththth/ **The** Continuous Voiced **Unit 10**	Hh /h/ **Hippo** Quick Unvoiced (not huh) **Unit 11**	Cc /c/ **Cat** Quick Unvoiced (not cuh) **Unit 12**	Rr /rrr/ **Rabbit** Continuous Voiced **Unit 13**	ea /eaeaea/ **Eagle** Continuous Voiced (Long) **Unit 13**
Sh/sh /shshsh/ **Sheep** Continuous Unvoiced **Unit 14**	Kk, -ck /k/ **Kangaroo** Quick Unvoiced (not kuh) **Unit 15**	oo /oooo/ **Moon** Continuous Voiced (Long) **Unit 16**	ar /ar/ **Shark** Voiced (R-Controlled) **Unit 17**	Wh/wh /wh/ **Whale** Quick Voiced **Unit 18**	Ee /ěěě/ **Engine or Ed** Continuous Voiced (Short) **Unit 19**
-y /-yyy/ **Fly** Continuous Voiced (Long) **Unit 20**	Ll /lll/ **Letter** Continuous Voiced **Unit 21**	Oo /ooo/ **Otter** Continuous Voiced (Short) **Unit 22**	Bb /b/ **Bat** Quick Voiced (not buh) **Unit 23**	all /all/ **Ball** Voiced **Unit 23**	Gg /g/ **Gorilla** Quick Voiced (not guh) **Unit 24**
Ff /fff/ **Frog** Continuous Unvoiced **Unit 25**	Uu /uuu/ **Umbrella** Continuous Voiced (Short) **Unit 26**	er /er/ **Sister** Voiced (R-Controlled) **Unit 27**	oo /oo/ **Book** Voiced (Short) **Unit 27**	Yy /y-/ **Yarn** Quick Voiced **Unit 28**	Aa /a/ **Ago** Voiced (Schwa) **Unit 28**
Pp /p/ **Pig** Quick Unvoiced (not puh) **Unit 29**	ay /ay/ **Hay** Voiced **Unit 29**	Vv /vvv/ **Volcano** Continuous Voiced **Unit 30**	Qu/qu /qu/ **Quake** Quick Unvoiced **Unit 31**	Jj /j/ **Jaguar** Quick Voiced (not juh) **Unit 32**	Xx /ksss/ **Fox** Continuous Unvoiced **Unit 33**
or /or/ **Horn** Voiced (R-Controlled) **Unit 33**	Zz /zzz/ **Zebra** Continuous Voiced **Unit 34**	a_e /a_e/ **Cake** Bossy E Voiced (Long) **Unit 34**	-y /-y/ **Baby** Voiced **Unit 35**	i_e /i_e/ **Kite** Bossy E Voiced (Long) **Unit 35**	ou /ou/ **Cloud** Voiced **Unit 36**
ow /ow/ **Cow** Voiced **Unit 36**	Ch/ch /ch/ **Chicken** Quick Unvoiced **Unit 37**	ai /ai/ **Rain** Voiced (Long) **Unit 37**	igh /igh/ **Flight** Voiced (Long) **Unit 38**	o_e /o_e/ **Bone** Bossy E Voiced (Long) **Unit 38**	ir /ir/ **Bird** Voiced (R-Controlled) **Unit 38**

Introduction

Flight

Theme Notes

With the theme of flight, celebrate students' accomplishments! Symbolically, the students—like the Wright brothers—have learned to fly. Ask students where they would like to travel. Begin exploring books that will take them where they'd like to go. When children read well, there are no boundaries.

In this unit, study the history of flight—from the dreams of the Greeks to hot air balloons, gliders, planes, jets, and spaceships. Students can do research, write reports, and build gliders.

Recommended Read Aloud

For reading outside of small group instruction

The Glorious Flight **by Alice and Martin Provensen**

Fiction • Narrative, Caldecott Award Winner

The year is 1901. Clacketa, clacketa, clacketa—the sounds of an early airship enchant a Frenchman named Louis Bleriot. He says, "I, too, will build a flying machine. A great white bird!" Later, despite a broken rib, a black eye, breaks, sprains, and bruises, Bleriot becomes the first person to cross the English Channel by air—demonstrating to the world that travel high over land and sea is possible. *The Glorious Flight* is a story of dreams and determination.

Read Well Connection

In the *Read Well* Storybook, students learn about hopes of flight from early Greek mythology to the first hot air balloon, and finally to the Wright brothers' first flight.

NOTE FROM THE AUTHORS

Early success in reading has been shown to be a strong predictor of later success in school. At the end of Unit 38, children have a strong foundation in the skills they need for a lifetime of reading.

New and Important Objectives

A Research-Based Reading Program

Just Right for Young Children

Oral Language
Phonemic Awareness
Phonics
Fluency
Vocabulary
Comprehension

◆◆ Oral Language

In Units 21–38, language patterns are provided for high-frequency words and for some of the low-frequency words that are likely to require clarification.

Phonemic Awareness

Isolating Beginning, Middle, Ending Sounds,
Segmenting, Blending, Rhyming, Onset and Rime

Phonics

Letter Sounds and Combinations

★*igh*, ★*o_e*, ★*ir*

Review • *Ss, Ee, ee, Mm, Aa, Dd, th, Nn, Tt, Ww, Ii, Th, Hh, Cc, Rr, ea, sh, Sh, Kk, -ck, oo, ar, wh, Wh,* e (short), *-y* (as in "fly"), *Ll, Oo, Bb, all, Gg, Ff, Uu, er, oo* (as in "book"), *Yy, a* (schwa), *Pp, ay, Vv, Qq, Jj, Xx, or, Zz, a_e, -y* (as in "baby"), *i_e, ou, ow, ch, Ch, ai*

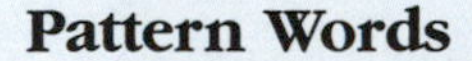

Pattern Words

★*Air*, ★*air*, ★*aircraft*, ★*airplane*, ★*airplanes*, ★*Airplanes*, ★*airplane's*, ★*alone*, ★*balloon*, ★*Balloon*, ★*balloons*, ★*Balloons*, ★*bird*, ★*birds*, ★*Birds*, ★*bright*, ★*brothers'*, ★*Channel*, ★*chapter*, ★*chirp*, ★*close*, ★*Close*, ★*Crumple*, ★*crumpled*, ★*dreamed*, ★*drift*, ★*drifted*, ★*drifts*, ★*drown*, ★*duck*, ★*eight*, ★*emu*, ★*experiment*, ★*Experiment*, ★*feathers*, ★*felt*, ★*fight*, ★*find*, ★*fire*, ★*first*, ★*five*, ★*flap*, ★*flat*, ★*flight*, ★*Flight*, ★*flying*, ★*fold*, ★*four*, ★*French*, ★*Frenchman*, ★*fright*, ★*frightened*, ★*frightening*, ★*girl*, ★*glide*, ★*glider*, ★*Glider*, ★*gliders*, ★*Gliders*, ★*glides*, ★*globe*, ★*Greeks*, ★*hail*, ★*hair*, ★*high*, ★*higher*, ★*hills*, ★*himself*, ★*History*, ★*holding*, ★*home*, ★*hope*, ★*hose*, ★*hotter*, ★*jets*, ★*keeps*, ★*lasted*, ★*leaps*, ★*learned*, ★*light*, ★*lightning*, ★*lighter*, ★*lit*, ★*locked*, ★*melting*, ★*might*, ★*model*, ★*motor*, ★*motors*, ★*movement*, ★*moves*, ★*night*, ★*nine*, ★*nose*, ★*pain*, ★*pair*, ★*paper*, ★*papers*, ★*pattern*, ★*plane*, ★*planes*, ★*powerful*, ★*rail*, ★*ready*, ★*ride*, ★*right*, ★*rocket*, ★*rode*, ★*rope*, ★*rose*, ★*sadly*, ★*Sadly*, ★*save*, ★*saved*, ★*seconds*, ★*seemed*, ★*sheet*, ★*ships*, ★*smiled*, ★*softly*, ★*sold*, ★*Sometimes*, ★*squirrel*, ★*squirrels*, ★*squirt*, ★*Step*, ★*stretches*, ★*Suddenly*, ★*surprised*, ★*teacher*, ★*testing*, ★*throw*, ★*throwing*, ★*thrust*, ★*Thrust*, ★*tower*,

◆◆ = Oral language patterns ★ = New in this unit

Pattern Words *(continued)*

★*trains,* ★*traveling,* ★*twelve,* ★*uses,* ★*wax,* ★*ways,* ★*Wright*

Review • *about, About, across, added, after, After, ago, all, also, an, An, and, arms, around, Ask, at, At, away, ball, be, began, big, but, by, called, can, cars, chain, Chapter, cold, day, did, didn't, different, down, dream, dripping, Drop, Each, eleven, ever, fall, fast, fear, fell, fifty, fly, foolish, for, For, found, fun, get, gets, getting, go, good, got, ground, had, hand, hands, happened, he, He, hear, help, hold, Hold, hood, hook, hot, Hot, how, How, hundred, hundreds, If, in, In, inside, it, It, its, jet, Jet, jumped, jumping, just, Just, land, last, lift, Lift, like, Like, long, look, looked, looking, lost, lots, made, make, man, me, moon, my, need, needs, no, not, Now, off, old, on, out, part, quickly, rain, real, room, rooster, round, same, sea, see, seem, seen, set, sets, seven, sheep, shouted, six, small, smaller, So, Soon, spent, started, Still, stood, story, Story, strong, such, sun, Sun, take, tell, tells, ten, than, that, That, them, Then, think, This, thousands, three, time, told, too, took, top, train, travel, traveled, tree, try, under, understand, until, up, way, we, went, when, When, which, Which, will, wind, wings, with, year, years, yelled*

Tricky Words

★*Americans,* ★*boy,* ★*doesn't,* ★*England,* ★*Englishman,* ★*Englishman's,* ★*forward,* ★*laughing,* ★*only,* ★*person,* ★*push,* ★*pushes,* ★*put,* ★*son,* ★*walk,* ★*watch,* ★*watched,* ★*world*

Review • *a, A, again, any, are, as, As, because, before, Before, brothers, Brothers, building, built, Come, could, couldn't, do, Do, does, English, everywhere, father, Father, from, give, gone, has, have, Have, his, His, I, into, is, island, legs, listen, listened, many, of, once, one, One, other, people, People, pretty, said, something, the, The, their, Their, there, There, they, They, to, Today, two, very, want, was, water, were, What, where, Where, who, Who, works, would, Would, Wouldn't, you, You, your, Your*

Comprehension

Comprehension Strategies

Building Knowledge, Priming Background Knowledge, Making Connections, Predicting, Identifying, Demonstrating, Defining, Applying, Explaining, Inferring, Classifying, Comparing, Responding, Visualizing, Questioning, Summarizing, Sequencing, Previewing

Story Elements

Title, Who (Character), Want (Goal), Problem, What (Action), Cause and Effect, Lesson

Story Vocabulary

★Flight, ★History, ★Experiment, ★Thrust, ★Lift, ★Glider, ★Hot Air Balloon, ★Jet

Text Structure

Beginning, Middle, End

Expository Elements

Fact, Topic Sentence, ★Chapter

Genre

Fiction • Traditional Myth (Adapted)

Nonfiction • Expository

Lessons

★Listen to your parents.

★Over the course of history, people have learned to fly.

Written Response

Sentence Illustration, Sentence Completion, List, Sentence Writing, Sentence Comprehension—Multiple Choice, Summarizing—Story Map, Conventions—Beginning Capital, Period

Fluency

Accuracy, Expression, Phrasing, Rate

Daily Lesson Planning

PACING

Some students will begin the process of learning to read slowly but make rapid progress later. If students complete Unit 38 by the end of the year, they will be at or above second grade level. Groups that are working at a slower pace may require more intensive *Read Well* instruction and practice. (See *Getting Started: A Guide to Implementation*.)

WEAK PASS CAUTION

If a student or students receive a Weak Pass on the previous two units, do not simply continue forward. See "Making Decisions" for Intervention Options.

ASSESSMENT

Upon completion of this unit, assess each student and proceed to *Read Well Plus* as appropriate.

SAMPLE LESSON PLANS

The sample lesson plans illustrate how materials can be used for students with different learning needs. Each lesson plan is designed to provide daily decoding practice and story reading.

3-DAY PLAN		
Day 1	**Day 2**	**Day 3**
• Decoding Practice 1 • Stories 1 and 2 • Comprehension Work 1* • Comprehension Work 2* • Homework 1, Story 1* • Homework 2, Story 2*	• Decoding Practice 2 • Stories 3 and 4 • Comprehension Work 3* • Comprehension Work 4* • Homework 3, Story 3*	• Decoding Practice 3 • Stories 5 and 6 • Comprehension Work 5* • Comprehension Work 6* • Homework 4, Story 4*

4-DAY PLAN			
Day 1	**Day 2**	**Day 3**	**Day 4**
• Decoding Practice 1 • Stories 1 and 2 • Comprehension Work 1* • Comprehension Work 2* • Homework 1, Story 1*	• Decoding Practice 2 • Stories 3 and 4 • Comprehension Work 3* • Comprehension Work 4* • Homework 2, Story 2*	• Decoding Practice 3 • Stories 5 and 6 • Comprehension Work 5* • Homework 3, Story 3*	• Decoding Practice 4 • Review Stories 3, 4, 5, and 6 • Comprehension Work 6* • Homework 4, Story 4*

* From *Read Well* Comprehension and Skill Work (workbook), *Read Well* Homework (blackline masters), or Extra Practice in this book.

6-DAY PLAN		
Day 1 • Decoding Practice 1 • Story 1 • Comprehension Work 1*	**Day 2** • Review Decoding Practice 1 • Story 2 • Comprehension Work 2* • Homework 1, Story 1*	**Day 3** • Decoding Practice 2 • Story 3 • Comprehension Work 3* • Homework 2, Story 2*
Day 4 • Review Decoding Practice 2 • Story 4 • Comprehension Work 4* • Homework 3, Story 3*	**Day 5** • Decoding Practice 3 • Story 5 • Comprehension Work 5* • Homework 4, Story 4*	**Day 6** • Decoding Practice 4 • Story 6 • Comprehension Work 6*

PRE-INTERVENTION AND INTERVENTION

See *Getting Started: A Guide to Implementation* for information on how to achieve mastery at a faster pace with students who require eight or more days of instruction.

8-DAY PLAN • *Pre-Intervention*			
Day 1 • Decoding Practice 1 • Story 1 • Comprehension Work 1*	**Day 2** • Review Decoding Practice 1 • Story 2 • Comprehension Work 2* • Homework 1, Story 1*	**Day 3** • Decoding Practice 2 • Story 3 • Comprehension Work 3*	**Day 4** • Review Decoding Practice 2 • Story 4 • Comprehension Work 4* • Homework 2, Story 2*
Day 5 • Decoding Practice 3 • Story 5 • Comprehension Work 5* • Homework 3, Story 3*	**Day 6** • Decoding Practice 4 • Story 6 • Comprehension Work 6* • Homework 4, Story 4*	**Day 7** • Extra Practice 1* • Extra Practice 1 Fluency Passage*	**Day 8** • Extra Practice 2* • Extra Practice 2 Fluency Passages*

10-DAY PLAN • *Intervention*				
Day 1 • Decoding Practice 1 • Story 1 • Comprehension Work 1*	**Day 2** • Review Decoding Practice 1 • Story 2 • Comprehension Work 2* • Homework 1, Story 1*	**Day 3** • Decoding Practice 2 • Story 3 • Comprehension Work 3*	**Day 4** • Review Decoding Practice 2 • Story 4 • Comprehension Work 4* • Homework 2, Story 2*	**Day 5** • Decoding Practice 3 • Story 5 • Comprehension Work 5* • Homework 3, Story 3*
Day 6 • Decoding Practice 4 • Story 6 • Comprehension Work 6* • Homework 4, Story 4*	**Day 7** • Extra Practice 1* • Extra Practice 1 Fluency Passage*	**Day 8** • Extra Practice 2* • Extra Practice 2 Fluency Passages*	**Day 9** • Extra Practice 3 • Extra Practice 3 Fluency Passage*	**Day 10** • Review Decoding Practice 4 • Review Solo Stories: Units 37–38

Materials and Materials Preparation

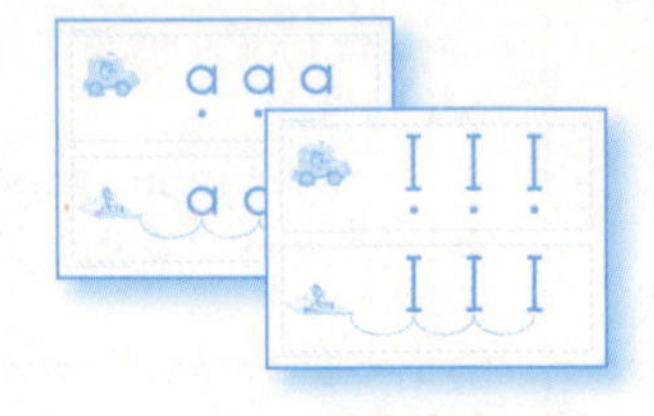

Core Lessons

Teacher Materials

READ WELL MATERIALS

- Unit 38 Teacher's Guide
- Sound and Word Cards 1–38
- *Assessment Manual* or pages 56 and 59

SCHOOL SUPPLIES

- Game markers (optional for use with cover-up activities)
- Stopwatch

Student Materials

READ WELL MATERIALS

- Decoding Book 4 for each student
- Unit 38 Storybook for each student
- Unit 38 Comprehension and Skill Work for each student (My Activity Book 4)
- Unit 38 Certificate of Completion (blackline master, page 57)
- Unit 38 Homework for each student

See *Getting Started* for suggested homework routines.

SCHOOL SUPPLIES

- Pencils, colors (optional—markers, crayons, or colored pencils)

Make one copy per student of each blackline master as appropriate for the group.

Note: For new or difficult Comprehension and Skill Work activities, make overhead transparencies from the blackline masters. Use the transparencies to demonstrate and guide practice.

Extra Practice Lessons

Note: Use these lessons only if needed.

Student Materials

READ WELL MATERIALS

- Unit 38 Extra Practice 1 and 2 for each student (blackline master pages 62 and 65)
- Unit 38 Extra Practice Fluency Passages 1, 2, and 3 for each student (blackline master pages 63, 66, and 68)

SCHOOL SUPPLIES

- Pencils, colors (markers, crayons, or colored pencils)
- White boards or paper

Concluding *Read Well 1*

Unit 38 represents the end of the core *Read Well 1* program.

COMPLETING *READ WELL 1*, UNIT 38

Upon completion, high-risk students consistently score at a 2.1 grade-level equivalency on standardized tests. Students with rich vocabulary and advanced thinking skills often score significantly higher.

END OF UNIT 38 ACCOMPLISHMENTS • PHONICS

Read Well students will have mastered the following skills:

Vowels and Vowel Patterns

e, ee, a, A, i, ea, oo (as in "moon"), *ar, e* (short), *E, -y* (as in "fly"), *o, O, all, u, U, er, oo* (as in "book"), *a* (schwa), *ay, or, a_e, -y* (as in "baby"), *i_e, ou, ow, ai, igh, o_e, ir*

Consonants

Mm, Ss, Dd, th, Nn, Tt, Ww, Th, Hh, Cc, Rr, sh, Sh, Kk, -ck, th (soft), *wh, Wh, Ll, Bb, Gg, Ff, Yy, Pp, Vv, Qq, Jj, Xx, Zz, ch, Ch*

Tricky Words (Irregular Words)

I, said, the, was, as, has, his, is, with, a, want, could, should, would, do, to, into, are, what, there, where, who, little, look, one, two, about, because, go, no, so, work, from, great, mother, other, say, school, were, word, America, father, often, you, your, animal(s), people, story, they, earth, even, give, have, live, of, very, been, come, some, more, something, water, before, another, any, many, their, again, don't, does, head, once, boy, four, learn(ed), only, put, walk, watch, world

Top 100 High-Frequency Words

Of the first 100 words on the Fry, Kress, and Fountoukidis (2000) Instant Words list, students have been introduced to all but five words: *use, these, write, number,* and *oil.*

END OF UNIT 38 ACCOMPLISHMENTS • FLUENCY

If *Read Well* has been implemented with fidelity, your students will be able to read the passage at right with 98% accuracy and a minimum fluency of 80 to 100 words correct per minute. Fluency is important because of its high correlation with comprehension.

STORY 3, SOLO

A History of Flight

CHAPTER 1

Hot Air Balloons

What is the title of this story? What does history tell us about? This story is about real things that happened long ago. Do you think the story is fact or fiction?

For thousands of years, people dreamed of traveling in the air like birds, but people had no way to fly. Then about two hundred years ago, two French brothers made a big balloon. They lit a small fire under the balloon and watched as the balloon rose in the air. Soon, their balloon was flying!

Would you like to understand how the hot air balloon could fly? Hot air is lighter than cold air. When the brothers lit the fire, the air inside the balloon got hotter. As the air got hotter, it got lighter, and the balloon began to fly. What do you think happened when the air in the balloon got cold?

The brothers put a rooster, a sheep, and a duck on the first flight of their balloon. Before long, many people rode in hot air balloons.

Who made the first hot air balloon? Pretend your hands are a balloon. Show me what happened to the balloon when the air got hot. Show me what happened when the air got cold. Two hundred years ago, no one had ever ridden in a hot air balloon before. Would you want to be the first one to try it? I think it would make me very nervous. If it didn't work, I wouldn't want anyone to get hurt!

9

END OF UNIT 38 ACCOMPLISHMENTS • COMPREHENSION AND WRITTEN RESPONSE

By the end of *Read Well 1*, children are able to complete oral retells and fact summaries. The page at right is a sample of the work your children will be doing in their Comprehension Work.

NEXT STEPS, FIRST GRADE

High-performing students are able to apply their skills to new contexts, and are able to induce new skills from their solid understanding of letter/sound associations, sounding out words, and word patterns. High-performing to average-performing students should complete *Read Well 1*, Unit 38 well before the end of first grade.

- By going into *Read Well Plus*, children are guaranteed continuous acceleration without program adaptation. Following *Read Well Plus*, students are typically able to work in a 2.2 (last half of a second grade program) basal reader.
- If *Read Well Plus* is not available, students can work in a 2.1 basal reading series, adapted to parallel the structure of a *Read Well* lesson. While continuously reviewing known letter sounds, systematically teach students *au, aw, ce, ci, ew, u_e, ge, gi, kn, oa, oi, ōw, oy, ph, ĕa,* and *-dge*. Base the sequence of sounds on passage vocabulary.

NEXT STEPS, SECOND GRADE

Low-average students are not able to generalize skills as easily in new contexts and need direct teaching of new skills. These students should complete *Read Well 1*, Unit 38 by the end of their first grade year.

- *Read Well Plus* is recommended for the beginning of second grade. Students can then work quickly through a 2.1 reader and into a 2.2 reader for the remainder of their second grade year.
- If *Read Well Plus* is not available, students can work in a 2.1 basal reading series, adapted to parallel the structure of a *Read Well* lesson.

Low-performing students require ongoing systematic direct instruction and repeated opportunities for extended practice. They often require time during their second grade year to complete *Read Well 1*, Unit 38. By going into *Read Well Plus*, these children are guaranteed continuous progress. Once *Read Well Plus* has been completed, these students should continue in a highly structured reading program.

How to Teach the Lessons

Teach from this section. Each instructional component is outlined in an easy-to-teach format. Special tips are provided to help you nurture student progress.

Decoding Practice 1

- Storybook Introduction
- Story 1, Solo
- Comprehension Work Activity 1
- Story 2, Solo
- Comprehension Work Activity 2

Decoding Practice 2

- Story Introduction
- Story 3, Solo
- Comprehension Work Activity 3
- Story 4, Solo
- Comprehension Work Activity 4

Decoding Practice 3

- Story 5, Solo
- Paper Glider Activity
- Comprehension Work Activity 5
- Story 6, Solo
- Glossary
- Comprehension Work Activity 6

Decoding Practice 4

Review Story 6 or Solo Stories from Units 37–38

BUILDING INDEPENDENCE

Next Steps • Principles of Instruction

As students complete *Read Well 1*, follow the scaffolded principles of instruction below.

Provide demonstration and/or guided practice only as needed with:

- New sounds
- New Tricky Words
- New multisyllabic words

Provide independent practice (practice without your assistance or voice) on:

- New and review pattern words with known sounds
- Review Tricky Words
- Review multisyllabic words

If students make errors, provide appropriate corrections.

- Have students identify any difficult sound and then sound out the word. Provide discrimination practice.
- Reintroduce difficult Tricky Words based on the initial introduction procedures.

If students require your assistance on words with known sounds, evaluate placement and consider a Jell-Well Review.

1 SOUND REVIEW

◆◆ FOR ENGLISH LANGUAGE LEARNERS AND CHILDREN WITH LANGUAGE DELAYS

Throughout Decoding Practice and Extra Practice, provide repeated use of the language patterns—both within and outside of lessons.

◆◆ 2 NEW SOUND INTRODUCTION

★ **New sound: /igh/**

- Tell students that i-g-h together say /igh/ as in "flight."
- After students read each word, quickly use the word in a sentence. *Flight* is movement through the air. When we talk about birds flying, we are talking about . . . (flight).

◆◆ 3 NEW SOUND INTRODUCTION

★ **New sound: /ir/**

- Remind students they know that e-r says /er/. Explain that i-r also says /er/.
- Have students read the sentence to themselves first, then read it aloud. Tell students they figured out how to say the word "feathers" using the sentence and the sounds they know.

◆◆ 4 SOUNDING OUT SMOOTHLY

★ **New sound: /o_e/ as in "bone"**

- Before students read this row, tell them to watch for the Bossy E. Remind them that it makes the underlined letter say its name. Help them with "close" if needed.
- Have students say the underlined part, sound out the word in one smooth breath, then read the word. Use each word in a sentence.
- Provide repeated practice, mixing group and individual turns on each word.

5 ACCURACY AND FLUENCY BUILDING

★ **New combination: /wa/**

- Tell students they know the first word in the Pencil Column. Have them say the underlined part, then read the word.
- Tell them the next two words begin with the same sound as "water." Before students read "walk," tell them the l is silent.
- Repeat practice on each column, building accuracy first and then fluency. Mix group and individual turns, independent of your voice.

6 STORY WORDS

7 MULTISYLLABIC WORDS

◆◆ 8 TRICKY WORDS

★ **New Tricky Words: "son," "boy," "put," "Only"**

- Have students try to figure out each of their new Tricky Words by themselves first. For each word, confirm or demonstrate the correct pronunciation and have students read the word several times.
- Use all the words in sentences and have students use the words in sentences.

9 DAILY STORY READING

Proceed to the Unit 38 Storybook. See Daily Lesson Planning for pacing suggestions.

10 COMPREHENSION AND SKILL WORK ACTIVITY 1 AND/OR ACTIVITY 2

See pages 17 and/or 22.

UNIT 38 DECODING PRACTICE 1
(For use with Stories 1 and 2)

1. SOUND REVIEW Use Sound Cards for Units 1–37.

★2. NEW SOUND INTRODUCTION Introduce /igh/ as in "high." For each word, have students say any underlined part, then read the word.

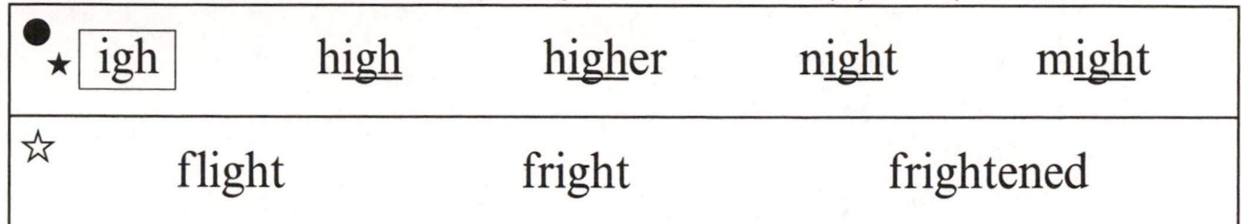

★3. NEW SOUND INTRODUCTION Introduce /ir/ as in "first." Have students say the underlined part and read each word, then read the sentence.

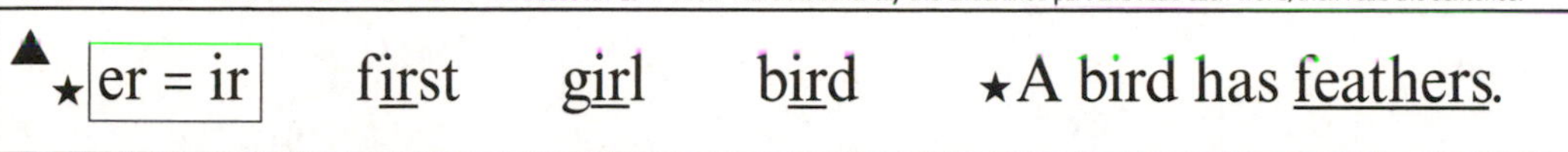

★4. SOUNDING OUT SMOOTHLY Have students say the underlined part, sound out the word in one smooth breath, then read the word.

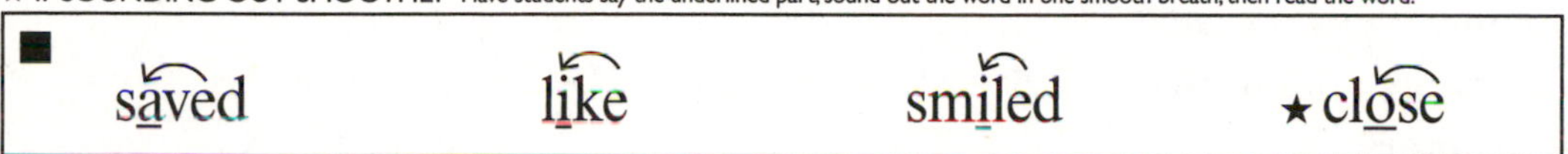

★5. ACCURACY/FLUENCY BUILDING For each column, have students say any underlined part, then read each word. Next have students practice the column.

♥	✎	✿	✈
old	★ water	each	look
told	watch	such	hook
cold	walk	which	hood
			stood

6. STORY WORDS Have students say any underlined part, then read the word.

7. MULTISYLLABIC WORDS Have students figure out each word silently and read it aloud.

★8. TRICKY WORDS See Teacher's Guide for how to introduce "son," "boy," "put," and "Only." Have students silently figure out each word and read it aloud.

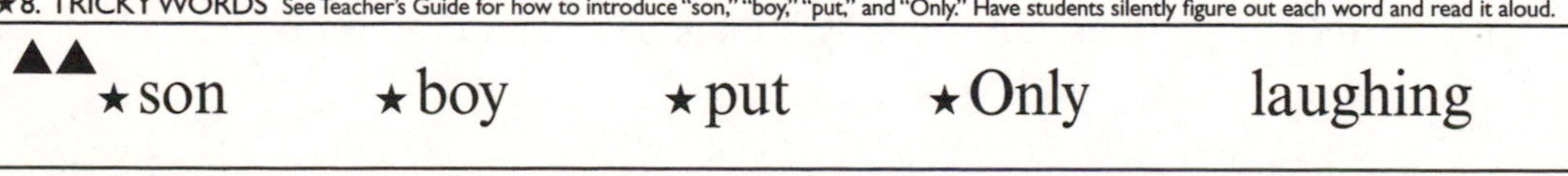

9. DAILY STORY READING

33

◆◆ SENTENCE SUGGESTIONS

● high – **Point to the [clock].** Look at the [clock]. It is too *high* to touch.

● night – We go to sleep at . . . *night*.

● might – When there are dark clouds in the sky, it . . . *might* rain.

☆ flight – *Flight* is movement through air. When we talk about birds flying, we are talking about . . . *flight*.

▲ first – [Marcos, Annie, and Bill], please line up next to me. Who is *first*?

▲ girl – Raise your hand if you are a *girl*. Yes, [Annie] is a girl. [Jess] is a girl, [and I am a girl].

■ close – We are sitting . . . *close* together. **Gesture.**

▲▲ son – The boy was his mother's *son*. The boy was his father's . . . (son).

▲▲ boy – Raise your hand if you are a *boy*.

▲▲ put – *Put* your hand on your head.

▲▲ Only – How many teachers are in this group? (One) There is one [teacher], so I'm the *only* teacher.

Sentence Suggestions: If a sentence is included, use it *after* decoding the individual word. The sentences may be used to build oral language patterns and vocabulary. Use of sentences also emphasizes that words have meaning.

❶ INTRODUCING THE STORYBOOK

Identifying—Title

Have students identify the title of the storybook.

Vocabulary—Flight

Remember *flight* is movement through the air.

When you are talking about birds flying, you are talking about *flight*.

When you are talking about airplanes, jets, and space shuttles flying, what are you talking about? (Flight)

Priming Background Knowledge

What do you already know about flight?

❷ USING THE TABLE OF CONTENTS

Identifying—What

Turn to page 2. This is the Table of Contents. The Table of Contents is a list of the stories and their page numbers.

Identifying—Title

This unit has two stories. What is the title of the first story? ("A Story of Flight")

Identifying—Chapters

The story is divided into two parts. Each part is called a chapter. How many chapters are in "A Story of Flight"? (Two)

Look at the Table of Contents. What chapter is on page 6?

Where would you look to find Chapter 2, "Too Close to the Sun"?

Vocabulary—History

The second story is called "A History of Flight."

History is the study of things that happened long ago.

❸ INTRODUCING VOCABULARY—TITLE PAGE

Vocabulary—Hot Air Balloon, Glider, Airplane

Turn to page 3 in your storybook. The vocabulary words are words you will learn more about in "A History of Flight."

Hot Air Balloon

A *hot air balloon* is an aircraft that uses hot air and wind to fly.

Glider

A *glider* is an aircraft that has no motor. A glider uses the movement of air to fly.

Airplane

An *airplane* is an aircraft that uses a motor to fly.

❹ INTRODUCING THE STORY

The first story in this unit is an old Greek story that was told hundreds of years ago—before people traveled in hot air balloons, gliders, or airplanes.

Think Aloud/Inferring

I wonder what made people want to fly. What do you think?

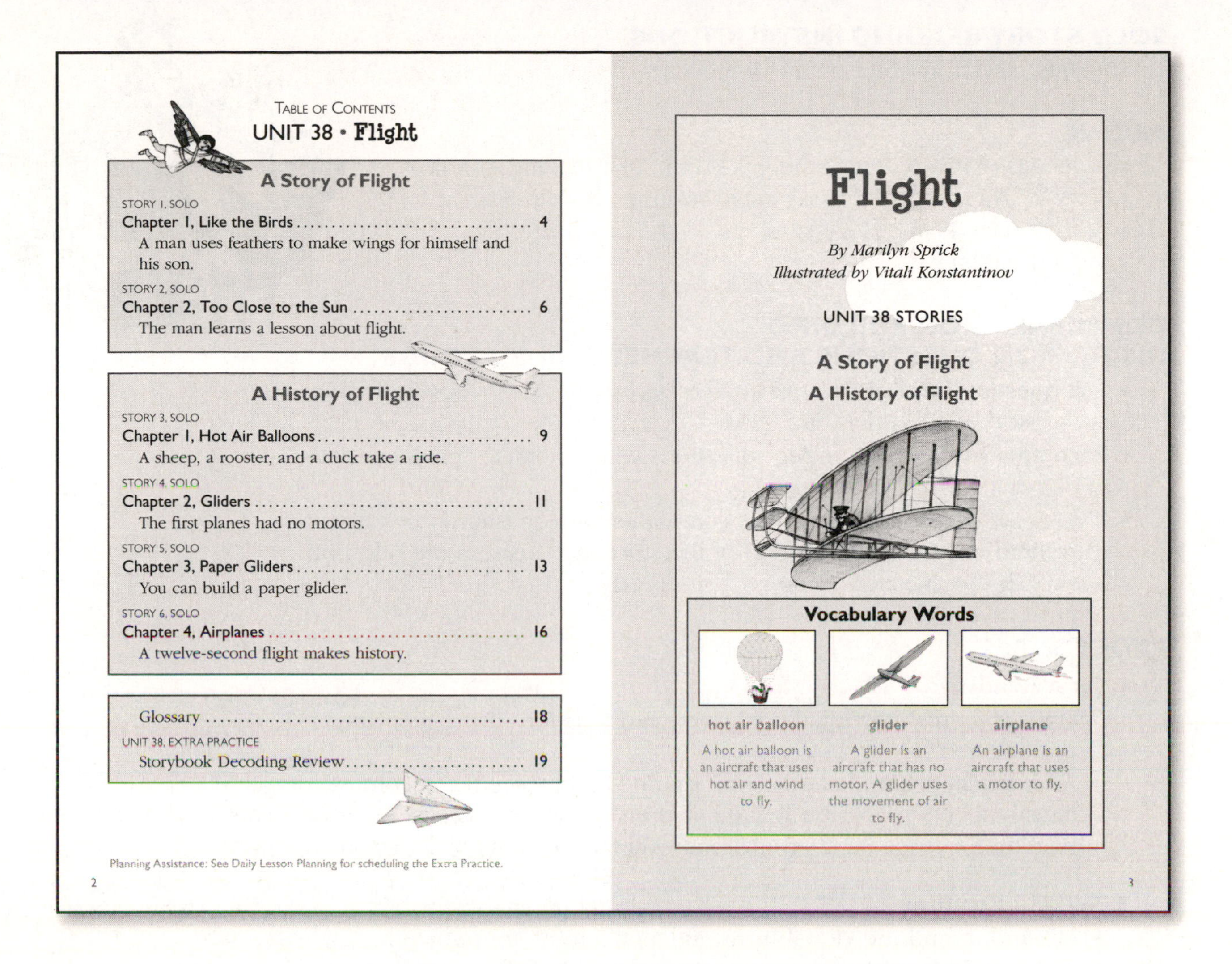

Table of Contents

UNIT 38 • Flight

Planning Assistance: See Daily Lesson Planning for scheduling the Extra Practice.

2

Flight

By Marilyn Sprick
Illustrated by Vitali Konstantinov

UNIT 38 STORIES

A Story of Flight
A History of Flight

Vocabulary Words

hot air balloon
A hot air balloon is an aircraft that uses hot air and wind to fly.

glider
A glider is an aircraft that has no motor. A glider uses the movement of air to fly.

airplane
An airplane is an aircraft that uses a motor to fly.

3

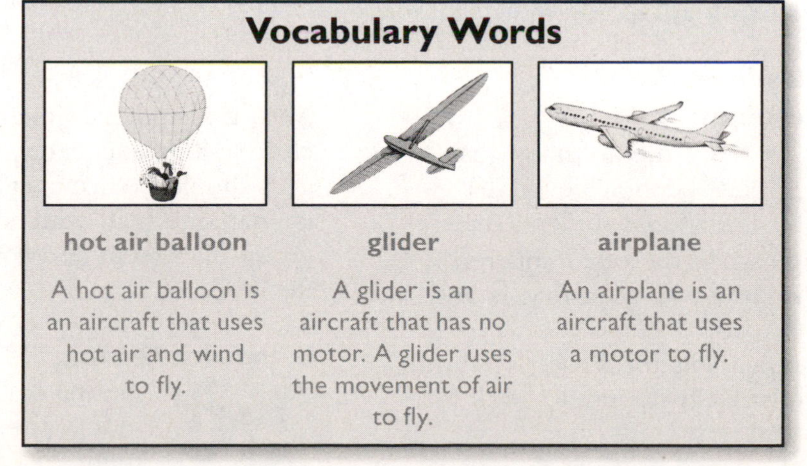

Vocabulary Words

hot air balloon
A hot air balloon is an aircraft that uses hot air and wind to fly.

glider
A glider is an aircraft that has no motor. A glider uses the movement of air to fly.

airplane
An airplane is an aircraft that uses a motor to fly.

Defining Vocabulary—Hot Air Balloon, Glider, Airplane

SOLO STORY READING INSTRUCTIONS

Students read from their own storybooks.

PACING

- 3- to 4-Day Plans: Have students do the first reading of Solo Story 1. Then proceed to repeated readings of Solo Story 2.
- 6- to 10-Day Plans: Have students do the first *and* second readings.

COMPREHENSION BUILDING: DISCUSSION QUESTIONS AND TEACHER THINK ALOUDS

- Ask questions and discuss text on the *second* reading when indicated in the storybook in light gray text.
- Encourage students to answer questions with complete sentences and to elaborate when appropriate.
- If students have difficulty with a comprehension question, think aloud with them or reread the portion of the story that answers the question. Then, ask the question again.

PROCEDURES

1. First Reading

- Have students individually whisper read the story using their fingers to track text.
- After students complete the first reading and before the second reading, have students practice a few paragraphs. First demonstrate expressive reading for students, then give individual turns. Acknowledge student efforts.

2. Second Reading

- Mix group and individual turns, independent of your voice. Have students work toward an accuracy goal of 0–2 errors. Quietly keep track of errors made by all students in each group.
- After reading the story, practice any difficult words.
- If the group has not reached the accuracy goal, have the group reread the story, mixing group and individual turns.

3. Repeated Readings

a. Timed Readings

- Once the accuracy goal has been achieved, have individual students read the page while the other children track the text with their fingers and whisper read. Time individuals for 30 seconds and encourage each student to work for a personal best.
- Count the number of words read correctly in 30 seconds (words read minus errors). Multiply by two to determine words correct per minute. Record student scores.

Note: If a student is unable to read with close to 100% accuracy, the personal goal should be accuracy. If the student is unable to read with accuracy, evaluate group placement and consider a Jell-Well Review.

b. Partner Reading

During students' daily independent work, have them do Partner Reading.

STORY 1, SOLO

A Story of Flight

CHAPTER 1

Like the Birds

Before there were cars and trains, people had to walk everywhere. They would watch the birds and dream of flying. Sometimes they would tell a story about flying.

The Greeks of long ago told such a story. A man and his son were locked in a tower on an island. Each day the man would watch the birds. When feathers fell from the birds, the man would save them. In time, he had saved hundreds of feathers.

The man added hot wax to the feathers. He made two sets of wings. He put one set of wings on himself and he put the other set on his son. Then the two went to the top of the tower and looked down at the sea.

The father said, "Each night I have dreamed about flying away. Now that it is time, I fear we might drown."

The boy smiled. "Do not be frightened, Father." Then he jumped from the tower.

4

Who are the two main characters in this Greek story?1 What problem did the man and his son have?2 What did they want?3 What did the man do?4 What happened at the end of this chapter?5

Look at the picture. The boy looks like he is having great fun.6 Do you think this story is fact or fiction?7 What do you think is going to happen next?8

5

1. **Identifying—Who** (A man and his son)
2. **Inferring—Problem** (They were locked in a tower.)
3. **Inferring—Goal** (They wanted to be free.)
4. **Identifying—Action** (He made wings.)
5. **Identifying—Action** (The man and his son put the wings on and went to the top of the tower. The man was afraid, but the boy jumped.)
6. **Teacher Think Aloud—Inferring**
7. **Classifying** (Fiction)
8. **Predicting**

STORY COMPREHENSION

Use work pages from the workbook.

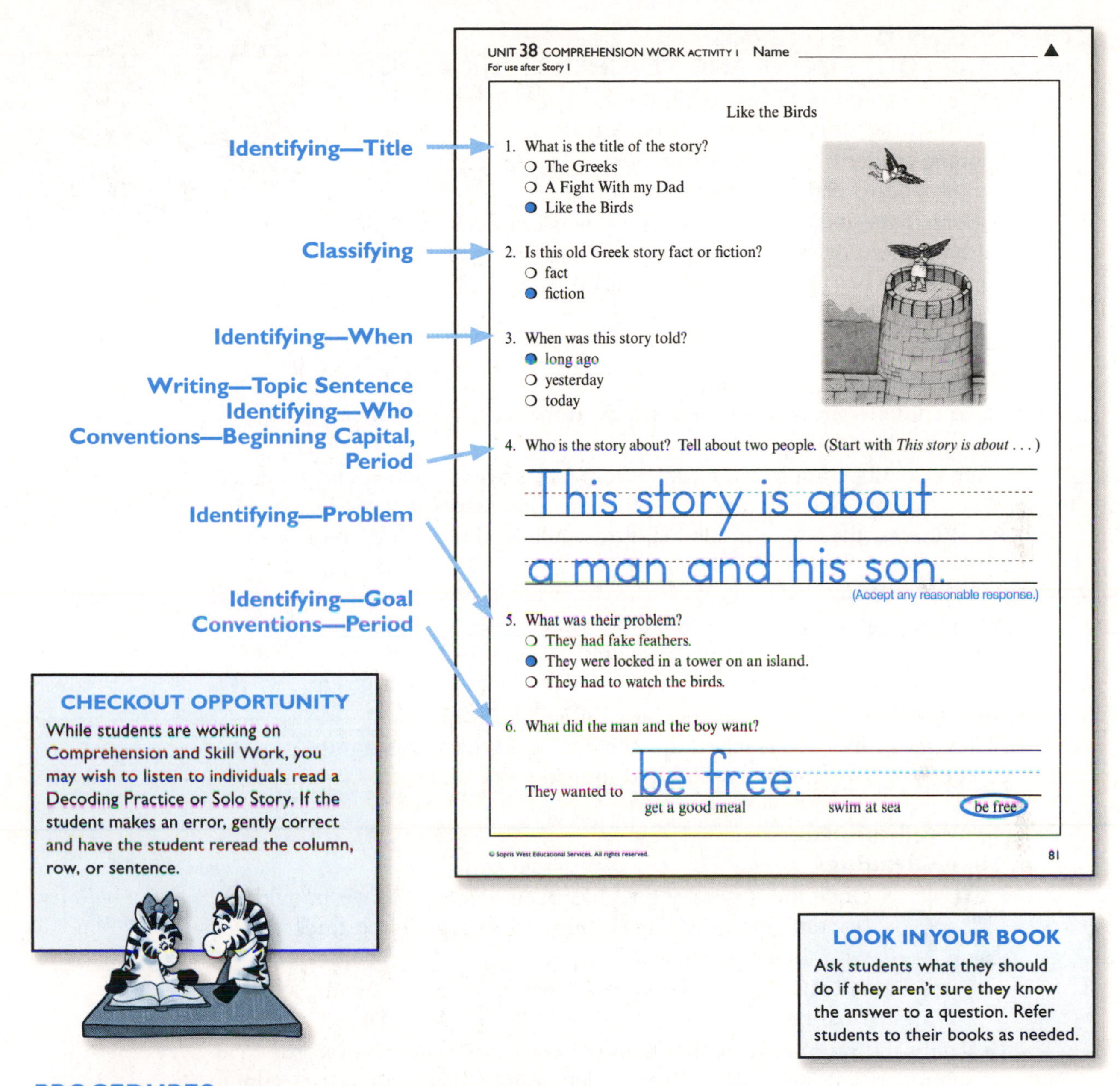

UNIT 38 COMPREHENSION WORK ACTIVITY 1 Name ______________________

For use after Story 1

Like the Birds

1. What is the title of the story?
   - ○ The Greeks
   - ○ A Fight With my Dad
   - ● Like the Birds

2. Is this old Greek story fact or fiction?
   - ○ fact
   - ● fiction

3. When was this story told?
   - ● long ago
   - ○ yesterday
   - ○ today

4. Who is the story about? Tell about two people. (Start with *This story is about . . .*)

   This story is about a man and his son.

   (Accept any reasonable response.)

5. What was their problem?
   - ○ They had fake feathers.
   - ● They were locked in a tower on an island.
   - ○ They had to watch the birds.

6. What did the man and the boy want?

   They wanted to be free.

   get a good meal   swim at sea   (be free)

81

CHECKOUT OPPORTUNITY

While students are working on Comprehension and Skill Work, you may wish to listen to individuals read a Decoding Practice or Solo Story. If the student makes an error, gently correct and have the student reread the column, row, or sentence.

LOOK IN YOUR BOOK

Ask students what they should do if they aren't sure they know the answer to a question. Refer students to their books as needed.

PROCEDURES

For each step, demonstrate and guide practice as needed.

1. Multiple Choice—Basic Instructions (Items 1, 2, 3, 5)

Have students fill in the bubble for the correct answer.

2. Sentence Writing—Basic Instructions (Item 4)

- Have students read the direction and brainstorm possible responses using complete sentences.
- Have students write a complete sentence that starts with a capital letter and ends with a period.

3. Multiple Choice, Sentence Completion—Basic Instructions (Item 6)

Have students read and circle the words that complete the sentence, then write the answer in the blank and end it with a period.

SOLO STORY READING INSTRUCTIONS

Students read from their own storybooks.

COMPREHENSION BUILDING: DISCUSSION QUESTIONS AND TEACHER THINK ALOUDS

- Ask questions and discuss text on the *second* reading when indicated in the storybook in light gray text.
- Encourage students to answer questions with complete sentences and to elaborate when appropriate.
- If students have difficulty with a comprehension question, think aloud with them or reread the portion of the story that answers the question. Then, ask the question again.

PROCEDURES

1. First Reading

- Have students individually whisper read the story, using their fingers to track text.
- After students complete the first reading and before the second reading, have students practice a paragraph. First demonstrate expressive reading for students, then give individual turns. Acknowledge student efforts.

2. Second Reading

- Mix group and individual turns, independent of your voice. Have students work toward an accuracy goal of 0–2 errors. Quietly keep track of errors made by all students in each group.
- After reading the story, practice any difficult words.
- If the group has not reached the accuracy goal, have the group reread the story, mixing group and individual turns.

3. Repeated Readings

a. Timed Readings

- Once the accuracy goal has been achieved, have individual students read the page while the other children track the text with their fingers and whisper read.

Time individuals for 30 seconds and encourage each student to work for a personal best.

- Count the number of words read correctly in 30 seconds (words read minus errors). Multiply by two to determine words correct per minute. Record student scores.

b. Partner Reading

During students' daily independent work, have them do Partner Reading.

c. Homework 1

Have students read the story at home. (A reprint of this story is available on a blackline master in *Read Well* Homework.)

STORY 2, SOLO

CHAPTER 2

Too Close to the Sun

Who is this story about?[1] What was the problem?[2] How were the boy and his father trying to get out of the tower?[3] What do you think will happen?[4]

The boy shouted, “Father, watch me fly like a bird.”

His father yelled, “Do not fly too high! Do not get too close to the sun!” But the boy did not listen.

Soon the man could hear his son laughing. The boy called out, “Come, Father! Come fly like a bird.” So the father began to fly too.

The boy was flying like a bird. Close your eyes. Imagine flying like a bird.[5] Show me what you would be doing with your wings.[6] Why do you think the father doesn't want his son to fly too high?[7]

6

1. **Identifying—Who** (A man and his son)
2. **Identifying—Problem** (They were locked in a tower.)
3. **Explaining** (By flying)
4. **Predicting**
5. **Visualizing**
6. **Demonstrating**
7. **Inferring**

STORY 2, SOLO

The boy had fun flying. He went higher and higher. The father called out again. "Do not fly too high! Do not get too close to the sun." Still the boy didn't listen.

What did the father say?[1] Did the boy listen?[2]

The boy looked down. His father seemed to be getting smaller and smaller. Suddenly, the boy felt hot wax dripping from his wings. The sun was melting the wax. The boy started to fall.

Why did the boy start to fall?[3]

7

❶ **Identifying—What** (He told his son not to fly too close to the sun.)
❷ **Inferring** (No)
❸ **Explaining** (The boy got too close to the sun and the wax that was holding his wings together melted.)

STORY 2, SOLO

The man could not help his son. He watched as the boy fell into the sea. Sadly, the man said, "If only my son had listened. I was foolish to want to fly. Now I have lost my son."

This was a sad story because the boy died. I'm glad it was fiction.[1] What should the boy have done?[2] What lesson do you think the author of this story was trying to teach us?[3]

8

CONFIRMING PREDICTIONS

After completing the story and questions, talk about the students' earlier predictions. Tailor your discussions to student predictions.

At the beginning of Chapter 2, some of us thought the boy and his father would fly home. Some of us thought the boy would finally listen to his father and fly lower. What really happened in the story was very sad. [Lindsey] thought something bad might happen because the boy didn't listen to his father. [Lindsey] was right.

1. **Teacher Think Aloud—Responding, Explaining**
2. **Inferring—Cause and Effect** (Listened to his father)
3. **Inferring—Lesson** (Listen to your parents.)

STORY MAP

Use work pages from the workbook.

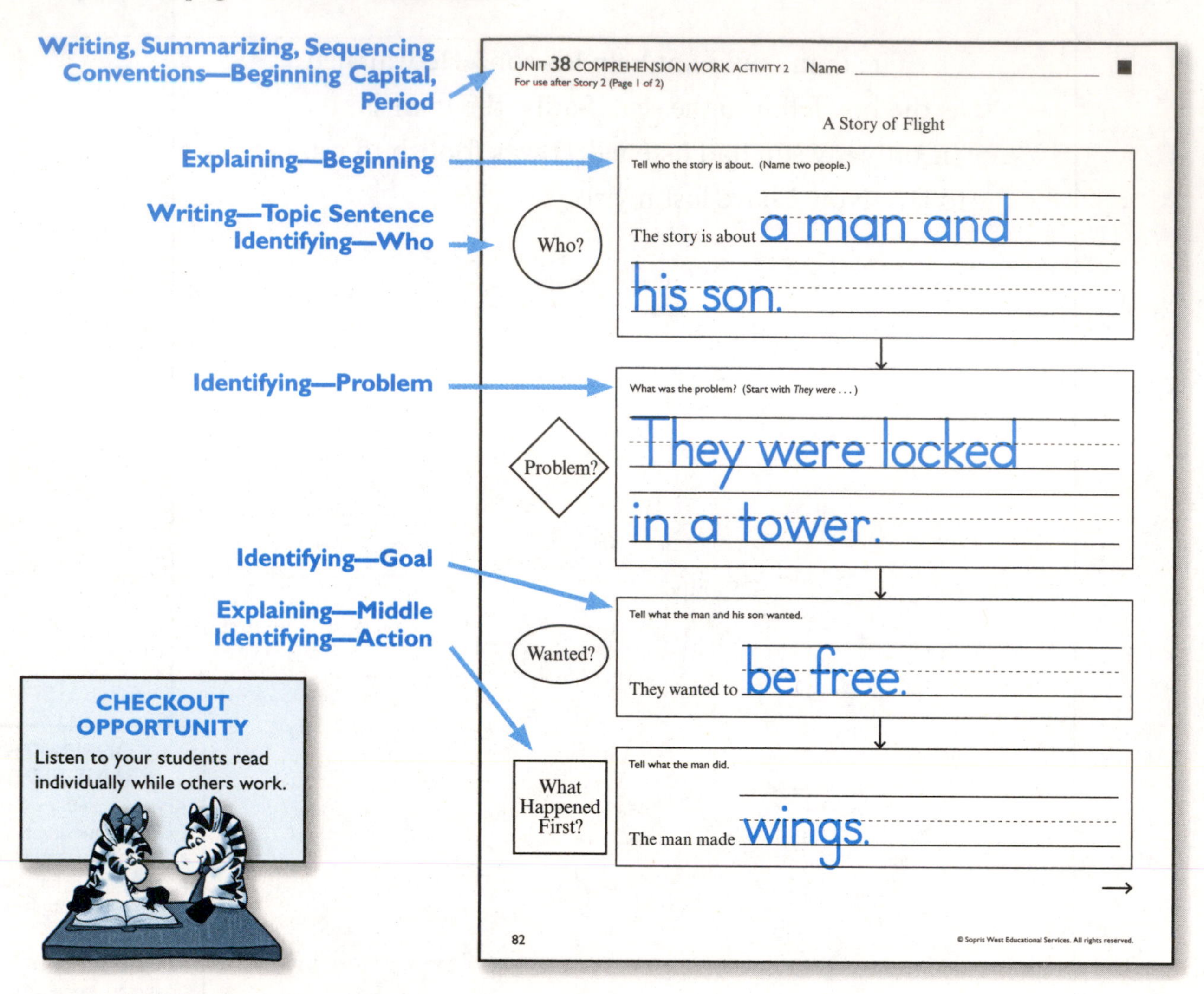

UNIT 38 COMPREHENSION WORK ACTIVITY 2 Name ____
For use after Story 2 (Page 1 of 2)

A Story of Flight

Who? — Tell who the story is about. (Name two people.)
The story is about a man and his son.

Problem? — What was the problem? (Start with *They were . . .*)
They were locked in a tower.

Wanted? — Tell what the man and his son wanted.
They wanted to be free.

What Happened First? — Tell what the man did.
The man made wings.

82

PROCEDURES

Story Map—Basic Instructions

- Using a blank or overhead copy of the story map from the blackline masters, help students identify the basic story elements—who the story is about, what the problem was, what the characters wanted, what happened in the story, and what happened at the end.
- Have students fill in the blanks to create a story map.
- Remind students that a story map helps them retell or summarize the important parts of a story.

Note: You may wish to remind students that a sentence begins with a capital and ends with a period.

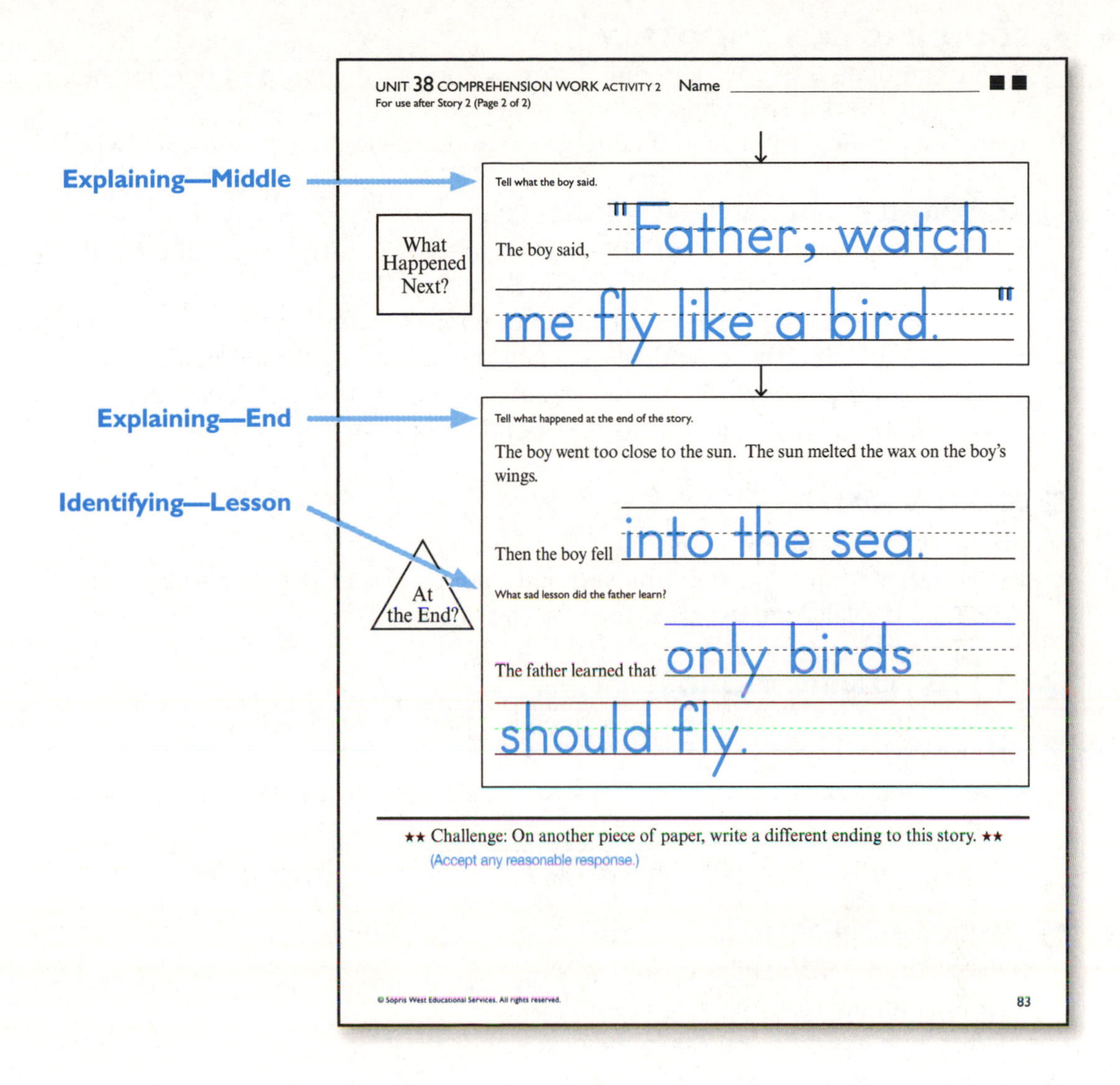
Explaining—Middle
Explaining—End
Identifying—Lesson
UNIT 38 COMPREHENSION WORK ACTIVITY 2 Name
For use after Story 2 (Page 2 of 2)
What Happened Next?
Tell what the boy said.
The boy said, "Father, watch me fly like a bird."
Tell what happened at the end of the story.
The boy went too close to the sun. The sun melted the wax on the boy's wings.
Then the boy fell into the sea.
At the End?
What sad lesson did the father learn?
The father learned that only birds should fly.
★★ Challenge: On another piece of paper, write a different ending to this story. ★★
(Accept any reasonable response.)
© Sopris West Educational Services. All rights reserved.
83

❶ SOUND REVIEW

◆◆ ❷ SOUNDING OUT SMOOTHLY

- Have students say any underlined part, sound out the word in one smooth breath, then read the word. Use each word in a sentence.
- Provide repeated practice, mixing group and individual turns on each word.

◆◆ ❸ ACCURACY AND FLUENCY BUILDING

- Before students read "stood" and "good" in the Heart Column, tell them that o-o in those words makes the same sound as it does in "look."
- Before students read the Pencil Column, remind them that they know what a-i says.
- For each column, have students say any underlined part, then read each word.
- Repeat practice on each column, building accuracy first and then fluency. Mix group and individual turns, independent of your voice.

❹ STORY WORDS

Focus on Vocabulary

Explain that "drifted" means "moved in a current of air." Say something like:

When the leaf fell from the tree, it drifted to the ground.

❺ MULTISYLLABIC WORDS

- You may wish to draw students' attention to the ir in "squirrels" before they read that word.
- Before students read the word "motor," tell them that the first part of the word rhymes with "go."
- If necessary, remind students that they have read the word "English" before.

◆◆ ❻ TRICKY WORDS

★ New Tricky Word: "person"

- After students read the word "son," ask:

  What little word do you see in the next new Tricky Word? (son)

  Right, what is your new word? (person)

  After students read the word, have them use it in a sentence.
- Have students read the row. Repeat, mixing group and individual turns, independent of your voice.

❼ DAILY STORY READING

Proceed to the Unit 38 Storybook. See Daily Lesson Planning pacing recommendations.

❽ COMPREHENSION AND SKILL WORK ACTIVITY 3 AND/OR ACTIVITY 4

See pages 31 and/or 35.

◆◆ For ELLs and children with language delays, provide repeated and extended practice with the language patterns.

UNIT 38 DECODING PRACTICE 2
(For use with Stories 3 and 4)

1. SOUND REVIEW Use Sound Cards for Units 1–38 or Sound Review on Decoding Practice 4.

2. SOUNDING OUT SMOOTHLY Have students say any underlined part, then read the word.

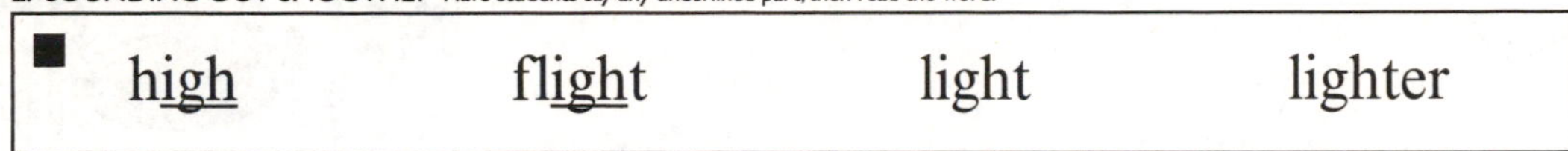

■	high	flight	light	lighter

3. ACCURACY/FLUENCY BUILDING For each column, have students say any underlined part, then read each word. Next have students practice the column.

♥	✏	✈	▲
old	rain	fire	home
cold	rail	ride	hope
stood	hail	glide	rode
good	hair	glider	round
	air		found

4. STORY WORDS Have students say any underlined part, then read the word.

●	birds	first	French	drifted

5. MULTISYLLABIC WORDS Have students figure out each word silently and read it aloud.

♥♥	softly	squirrels	rooster	motor
■■	England	Englishman	balloon	before

★6. TRICKY WORDS See Teacher's Guide for how to introduce "person." Next, have students silently figure out each word and read it aloud.

▲▲	does	son	★person	only	boy

7. DAILY STORY READING
34

◆◆ SENTENCE SUGGESTIONS

■ light – A piece of paper doesn't weigh very much. It is *light*. The opposite of heavy is . . . *light*.

✏ air – Mammals breathe . . . *air*.

✈ glider – An aircraft with no motor is called a . . . *glider*.

▲ home – Where you live is your . . . *home*.

▲▲ does – What does a [rooster] say?

Sentence Suggestions: Use the appropriate suggested sentence *after* decoding each individual word.

❶ INTRODUCING THE STORY—TABLE OF CONTENTS

Turn to page 2 in your storybook. We're going to start reading "A History of Flight." Find "A History of Flight" in the Table of Contents.

Vocabulary—History

History is the study of things that happened long ago.

Applying

Do you think people had planes long ago? (No)

Identifying—Chapters

How many chapters are in "A History of Flight"? (Four)

Let's read the chapters and their titles. Chapter 1, "Hot Air Balloons;" Chapter 2 . . .

Teacher Think Aloud—Responding

I think it is going to be interesting to study how people learned to fly.

Questioning

What would you like to learn about the history of flight?

Some of your questions will be answered when we read "A History of Flight."

If your questions aren't answered, we can look in other books to find out more about flight.

Identifying—Chapter

Find Chapter 1 in the Table of Contents.

What's the chapter title? ("Hot Air Balloons")

What page does Chapter 1 start on? (Page 9)

Turn to page 9.

Table of Contents

UNIT 38 • Flight

A Story of Flight

A History of Flight

Planning Assistance: See Daily Lesson Planning for scheduling the Extra Practice.

2

SOLO STORY READING INSTRUCTIONS

Students read from their own storybooks.

PACING

- 3- to 4-Day Plans: Have students do the first reading of Solo Story 3.
  Then proceed to repeated readings of Solo Story 4.
- 6- to 10-Day Plans: Have students do the first *and* second readings.

COMPREHENSION BUILDING: DISCUSSION QUESTIONS AND TEACHER THINK ALOUDS

- Ask questions and discuss text on the *second* reading when indicated in the storybook in light gray text.
- Encourage students to answer questions with complete sentences and to elaborate when appropriate.
- If students have difficulty with a comprehension question, think aloud with them or reread the portion of the story that answers the question. Then, ask the question again.

PROCEDURES

1. First Reading

- Have students individually whisper read the story, using their fingers to track text.
- After students complete the first reading and before the second reading, have students practice a paragraph. First demonstrate expressive reading for students, then give individual turns. Acknowledge student efforts.

2. Second Reading

- Mix group and individual turns, independent of your voice.
  Have students work toward an accuracy goal of 0–2 errors.
  Quietly keep track of errors made by all students in each group.
- After reading the story, practice any difficult words.
- If the group has not reached the accuracy goal, have the group reread the story, mixing group and individual turns.

3. Repeated Readings

a. Timed Readings

- Once the accuracy goal has been achieved, have individual students read the page while the other children track the text with their fingers and whisper read.
  Time individuals for 30 seconds and encourage each student to work for a personal best.
- Determine words correct per minute. Record student scores.

b. Partner Reading

During students' daily independent work, have them do Partner Reading.

c. Homework 2

Have students read the story at home. (A reprint of this story is available on a blackline master in *Read Well* Homework.)

STORY 3, SOLO

A History of Flight

CHAPTER 1

Hot Air Balloons

What is the title of this story? 1 What does history tell us about? 2 This story is about real things that happened long ago. Do you think the story is fact or fiction? 3

For thousands of years, people dreamed of traveling in the air like birds, but people had no way to fly. Then about two hundred years ago, two French brothers made a big balloon. They lit a small fire under the balloon and watched as the balloon rose in the air. Soon, their balloon was flying!

Would you like to understand how the hot air balloon could fly? Hot air is lighter than cold air. When the brothers lit the fire, the air inside the balloon got hotter. As the air got hotter, it got lighter, and the balloon began to fly. What do you think happened when the air in the balloon got cold?

The brothers put a rooster, a sheep, and a duck on the first flight of their balloon. Before long, many people rode in hot air balloons.

Who made the first hot air balloon? 4 Pretend your hands are a balloon. Show me what happened to the balloon when the air got hot. 5 Show me what happened when the air got cold. 6 Two hundred years ago, no one had ever ridden in a hot air balloon before. Would you want to be the first one to try it? 7 I think it would make me very nervous. If it didn't work, I wouldn't want anyone to get hurt! 8

9

1. **Identifying—Title** (A History of Flight)
2. **Using Vocabulary—History** (History is the study of things that happened long ago.)
3. **Classifying, Using Vocabulary—Fact, Fiction**
4. **Identifying—Who** (Two French brothers)
5. **Demonstrating—Cause and Effect**
6. **Demonstrating—Cause and Effect**
7. **Responding**
8. **Teacher Think Aloud—Explaining**

STORY 3, SOLO

What did the brothers put in their first hot air balloon?[1] Why do you think the brothers didn't ride in the balloon?[2]

10

MAKING CONNECTIONS

After completing the story, discuss the hot air balloons your students have seen.

Encourage the connections students make with prior knowledge by commenting on their reflections.

[Jonathan], you are right. People still fly in hot air balloons for fun. I've seen them near the farmland.

❶ **Identifying—What** (A sheep, a rooster, and a duck)

❷ **Inferring/Explaining** (They needed to find out if it would be safe.)

STORY COMPREHENSION

Use work pages from the workbook.

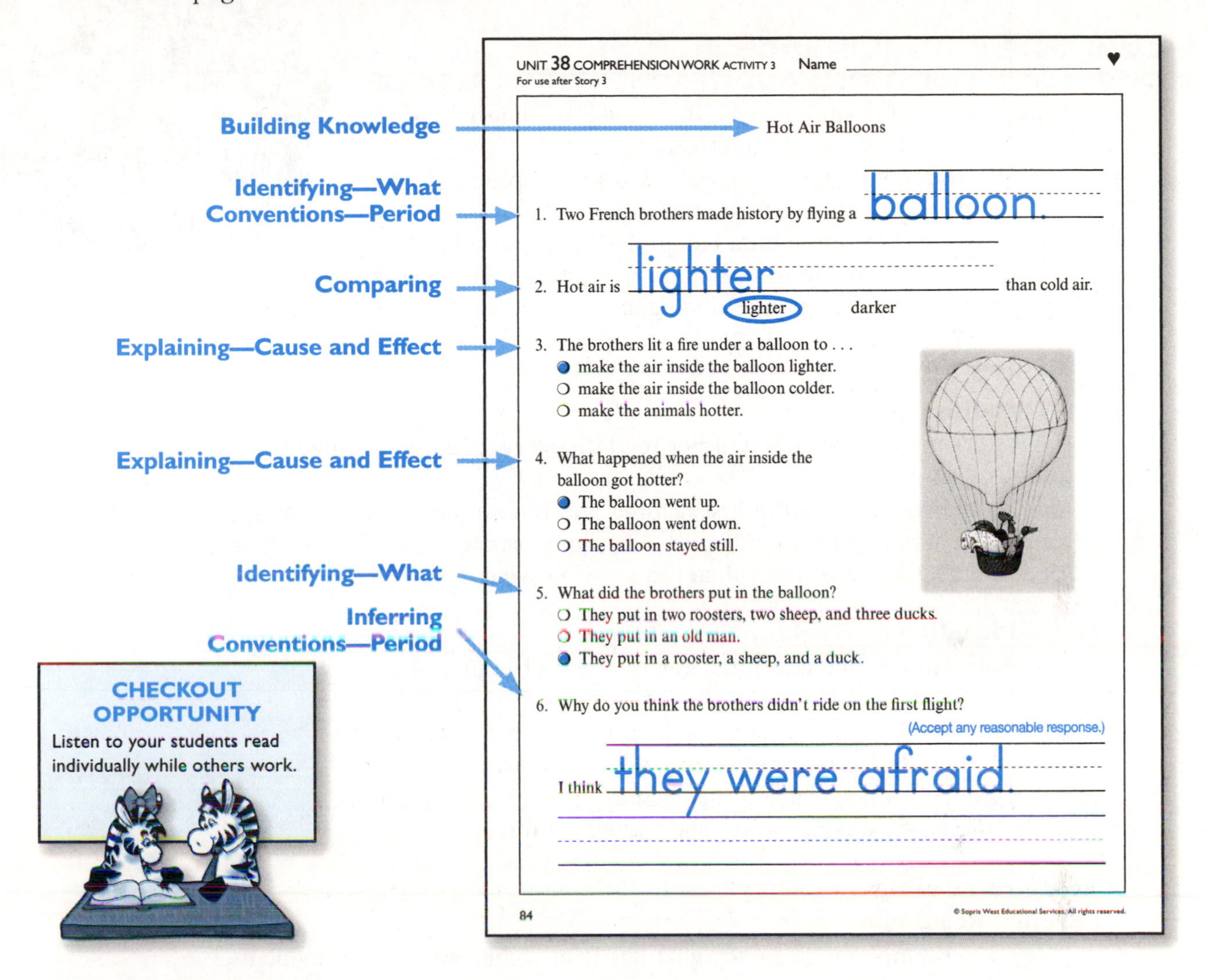

PROCEDURES

For each step, demonstrate and guide practice as needed.

1. Sentence Completion—Basic Instructions (Item 1)

Have students read and complete the sentence, then end it with a period.

2. Multiple Choice, Sentence Completion—Basic Instructions (Item 2)

Have students select and circle the word that correctly completes the sentence, then write the answer in the blank.

3. Multiple Choice—Basic Instructions (Item 3, 4, 5)

Have students fill in the bubble for the correct answer.

4. Sentence Writing—Basic Instructions (Item 6)

- Have students read the direction and brainstorm possible responses using complete sentences.
- Have students write a complete sentence that ends with a period.

SOLO STORY READING INSTRUCTIONS

Students read from their own storybooks.

COMPREHENSION BUILDING: DISCUSSION QUESTIONS AND TEACHER THINK ALOUDS

- Ask questions and discuss text on the *second* reading when indicated in the storybook in light gray text.
- Encourage students to answer questions with complete sentences and to elaborate when appropriate.
- If students have difficulty with a comprehension question, think aloud with them or reread the portion of the story that answers the question. Then, ask the question again.

PROCEDURES

1. First Reading

- Have students individually whisper read the story, using their fingers to track text.
- After students complete the first reading and before the second reading, have students practice a paragraph. First demonstrate expressive reading for students, then give individual turns. Acknowledge student efforts.

2. Second Reading

- Mix group and individual turns, independent of your voice. Have students work toward an accuracy goal of 0–2 errors. Quietly keep track of errors made by all students in each group.
- After reading the story, practice any difficult words.
- If the group has not reached the accuracy goal, have the group reread the story, mixing group and individual turns.

3. Repeated Readings

a. Timed Readings

- Once the accuracy goal has been achieved, have individual students read the page while the other children track the text with their fingers and whisper read.

Time individuals for 30 seconds and encourage each student to work for a personal best.

- Count the number of words read correctly in 30 seconds (words read minus errors). Multiply by two to determine words correct per minute. Record student scores.

b. Partner Reading

During students' daily independent work, have them do Partner Reading.

c. Homework 2

Have students read the story at home. (A reprint of this story is available on a blackline master in *Read Well* Homework.)

STORY 4, SOLO

CHAPTER 2

Gliders

This is another story about the *history* of flight. What does the word "history" tell us?1 In our last story, what did people try flying in?2 In this story, you will find out why people looked for other ways to fly and what they tried next.3

In time, people found that hot air balloons were not a good way to travel. The balloons could only go where the wind took them. So, people started looking for other ways to fly.

Have you ever seen a flying squirrel? A flying squirrel does not fly like a bird. It leaps from a tree into the air and stretches out its arms and legs. The squirrel does not flap its arms and legs. It just drifts softly to the ground. The flying squirrel glides.

Look at the picture. Now, close your eyes. Imagine that you are a flying squirrel.4 Hold out your arms and imagine drifting gently to the ground.5

1. **Defining Vocabulary** (This is about long ago.)
2. **Priming Background Knowledge** (Hot air balloons)
3. **Previewing**
4. **Visualizing**
5. **Demonstrating**

STORY 4, SOLO

About one hundred fifty years ago, people began to fly in gliders. Gliders are planes with wings and no motors. They drift softly in the air—just like a flying squirrel.

Gliders have to take off from high ground, such as the tops of hills. The first person who made a glider was an old man from England. The first person who rode in the Englishman's glider was a ten-year-old boy!

Let's review some facts that we learned about gliders. **1** When did people begin flying in gliders? **2** How are gliders different from planes? **3** Who was the first person to make a glider? **4** Who was the first person to ride in a glider? **5** Why do you think the old man had a boy ride in the glider? **6**

12

1. **Summarizing—Facts**
2. **Identifying—When** (150 years ago)
3. **Comparing** (Gliders do not have motors.)
4. **Identifying—Who** (An old man from England)
5. **Identifying—Who** (A boy)
6. **Inferring** (I wonder if it had something to do with how light the boy was.)

STORY COMPREHENSION

Use work pages from the workbook.

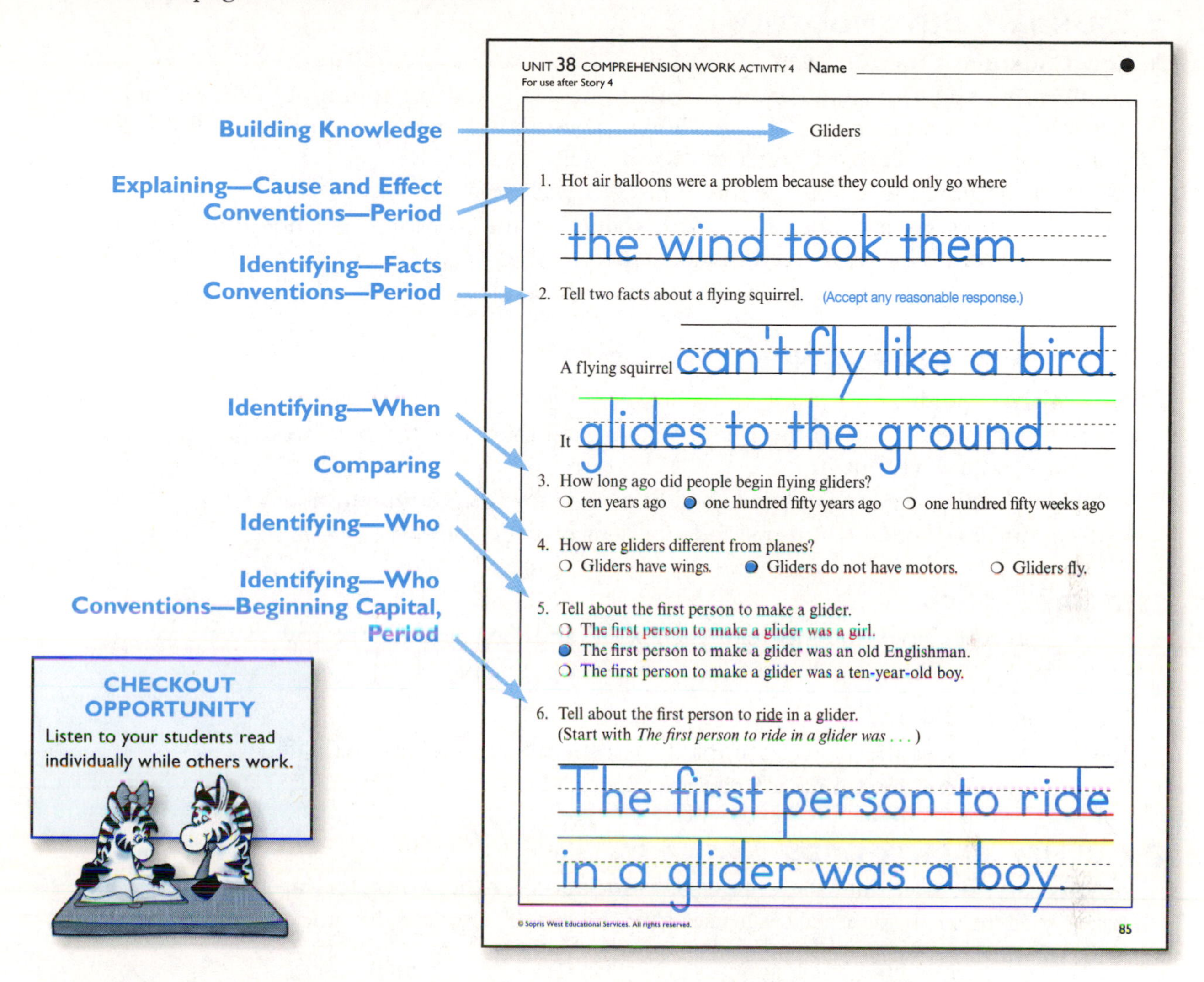

Building Knowledge

Explaining—Cause and Effect
Conventions—Period

Identifying—Facts
Conventions—Period

Identifying—When

Comparing

Identifying—Who

Identifying—Who
Conventions—Beginning Capital, Period

CHECKOUT OPPORTUNITY
Listen to your students read individually while others work.

UNIT 38 COMPREHENSION WORK ACTIVITY 4 Name ____________
For use after Story 4

Gliders

1. Hot air balloons were a problem because they could only go where
the wind took them.

2. Tell two facts about a flying squirrel. (Accept any reasonable response.)
A flying squirrel can't fly like a bird.
It glides to the ground.

3. How long ago did people begin flying gliders?
❍ ten years ago ● one hundred fifty years ago ❍ one hundred fifty weeks ago

4. How are gliders different from planes?
❍ Gliders have wings. ● Gliders do not have motors. ❍ Gliders fly.

5. Tell about the first person to make a glider.
❍ The first person to make a glider was a girl.
● The first person to make a glider was an old Englishman.
❍ The first person to make a glider was a ten-year-old boy.

6. Tell about the first person to ride in a glider.
(Start with *The first person to ride in a glider was . . .*)
The first person to ride in a glider was a boy.

© Sopris West Educational Services. All rights reserved. 85

PROCEDURES

For each step, demonstrate and guide practice as needed.

1. Sentence Completion—Basic Instructions (Item 1)
Have students read and complete the sentence, then end it with a period.

2. Sentence Writing—Basic Instructions (Items 2, 6)
- Have students read the direction and brainstorm possible responses using complete sentences.
- Have students write a complete sentence that begins with a capital and ends with a period, as appropriate.

3. Multiple Choice—Basic Instructions (Items 3, 4, 5)
Have students fill in the bubble for the correct answer.

❶ SOUND REVIEW

❷ SOUNDING OUT SMOOTHLY

★ **New Consonant Blend: /Wr-/**

The W-r in "Wright" can almost be sounded out. After students sound out "Wright," tell them that this word is a last name. If time allows, have students practice reading the following words from the chalkboard: "wreck," "wrong," and "wrist."

Ask students how the words are the same. (They all begin with w-r.)

- Have students say any underlined part, sound out the word in one smooth breath, then read the word. Use each word in a sentence.
- Repeat, mixing group and individual turns, independent of your voice.

◆◆ ❸ ACCURACY AND FLUENCY BUILDING

★ **New Word: "push"**

After students read "put" in the Heart Column, tell them that the next word has the same beginning sound as "put."

- Repeat practice on each column, building accuracy first and then fluency.
- Mix group and individual turns, independent of your voice.

❹ STORY WORDS

- For each row, have students read each word and then practice the row.
- Mix group and individual turns, independent of your voice.

Focus on Vocabulary

After students read the word "crumpled," tell them that it means "wrinkled."

Show them a crumpled piece of paper.

❺ MULTISYLLABIC WORDS

If necessary, demonstrate the correct pronunciation for the word "forward."

Ask a student to show you how to walk backward. Then have the student show you how to walk forward.

Focus on Vocabulary

- Tell students that an experiment is a test to prove something.
  Say something like:
  In science, we might do an experiment.
- Review any experiments students have conducted in science.

❻ TRICKY WORDS

❼ DAILY STORY READING

Proceed to the Unit 38 Storybook. See Daily Lesson Planning pacing recommendations.

❽ COMPREHENSION AND SKILL WORK ACTIVITY 5 AND/OR ACTIVITY 6

See pages 45 and/or 50.

◆◆ For ELLs and children with language delays, provide repeated and extended practice with the language patterns.

UNIT 38 DECODING PRACTICE 3
(For use with Stories 5 and 6)

1. SOUND REVIEW Use Sound Cards for Units 1–38 or Sound Review on Decoding Practice 4.

★2. SOUNDING OUT SMOOTHLY Have students say any underlined part, then read the word.

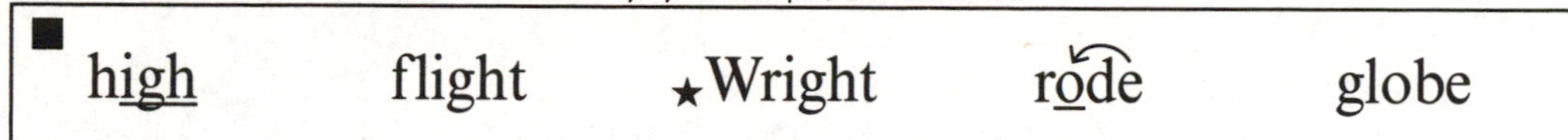

■ high	flight	★Wright	rode	globe

★3. ACCURACY/FLUENCY BUILDING For each column, have students read each word. Next have students practice the column.

♥		
air	old	lift
airplane	cold	drift
put	hold	just
★push	holding	thrust

4. STORY WORDS Have students read each word and then practice the row.

● built	building	teacher	crumpled
●● pattern	jumping	gliders	squirrel

5. MULTISYLLABIC WORDS Have students say each word part, then read the whole word.

▲ for•ward = forward	ex•per•i•ment = experiment
▲▲ a•lone = alone	a•bout = about

6. TRICKY WORDS Have students silently figure out each word and then read it aloud.

■■ only	their	doesn't	Once

7. DAILY STORY READING

35

◆◆ **SENTENCE SUGGESTIONS**

♥ push – Watch me *push* my chair back. Now you carefully push your chair back.

● crumpled – In our experiment, we will use a *crumpled* piece of paper. **Show students a crumpled piece of paper.** This is a . . . *crumpled* piece of paper.

●● gliders – Aircraft that fly without motors are called . . . *gliders*.

▲ forward – Watch me lean *forward*. Now you lean forward.

▲ experiment – Scientists try to find the answers to questions by running tests. A test is called an *experiment*. In Chapter 3 of our story we are going to run an experiment.

Sentence Suggestions: Use the appropriate suggested sentence *after* decoding each individual word.

SOLO STORY READING INSTRUCTIONS

Students read from their own storybooks.

PACING

- 3- to 4-Day Plans: Have students do the first reading of Solo Story 5. Then proceed to repeated readings of Solo Story 6.
- 6- to 10-Day Plans: Have students do the first *and* second readings.

COMPREHENSION BUILDING: DISCUSSION QUESTIONS AND TEACHER THINK ALOUDS

- Ask questions and discuss text on the *second* reading when indicated in the storybook in light gray text.
- Encourage students to answer questions with complete sentences and to elaborate when appropriate.
- If students have difficulty with a comprehension question, think aloud with them or reread the portion of the story that answers the question. Then, ask the question again.

PROCEDURES

1. First Reading

- Have students individually whisper read the story, using their fingers to track text.
- After students complete the first reading and before the second reading, have students practice a paragraph. First demonstrate expressive reading for students, then give individual turns. Acknowledge student efforts.

2. Second Reading

- Mix group and individual turns, independent of your voice. Have students work toward an accuracy goal of 0–2 errors. Quietly keep track of errors made by all students in each group.
- After reading the story, practice any difficult words.
- If the group has not reached the accuracy goal, have the group reread the story, mixing group and individual turns.

3. Repeated Readings

a. Timed Readings

- Once the accuracy goal has been achieved, have individual students read the page while the other children track the text with their fingers and whisper read.
  Time individuals for 30 seconds and encourage each student to work for a personal best.
- Determine words correct per minute. Record student scores.

b. Partner Reading

During students' daily independent work, have them do Partner Reading.

c. Homework 3

Have students read the story at home. (A reprint of this story is available on a blackline master in *Read Well* Homework.)

SPECIAL NOTE: GLIDER PROJECT

See page 42 for paper glider instructions and a pattern. Before having students make and fly their own gliders, follow the preparation procedures.

STORY 5, SOLO

CHAPTER 3

Paper Gliders

How is a glider different than an airplane?[1] This story has an experiment in it. What do scientists do when they experiment?[2]

Gliders are different from airplanes because they have no motors. You can make a glider out of paper. This experiment will help you understand how a paper glider works.

Experiment

Step 1. Crumple a sheet of paper into a ball. Hold the crumpled ball in one hand.

Step 2. In your other hand, hold a flat sheet of paper.

Step 3. Hold your hands as high as you can.

Step 4. Drop the two papers at the same time.

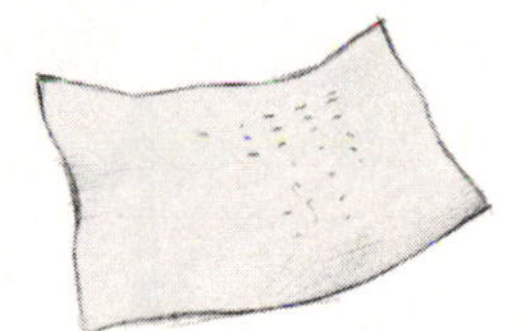

13

1 **Comparing** (A glider has no motor.)

2 **Defining Vocabulary—Experiment** (They try to find an answer by running a test.)

STORY 5, SOLO

Which sheet of paper fell to the ground quickly?

Which sheet of paper drifted softly to the ground?

I wonder why both sheets of paper don't land on the ground at the same time.1 What do you think?2

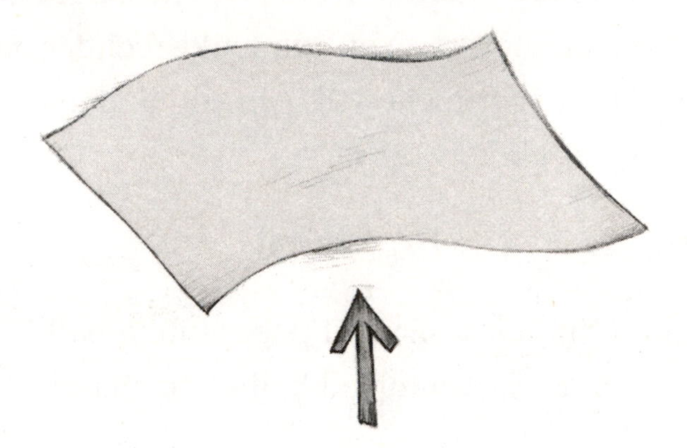

Air pushes up under the flat paper. This is called lift. A paper glider needs flat wings to give it lift.

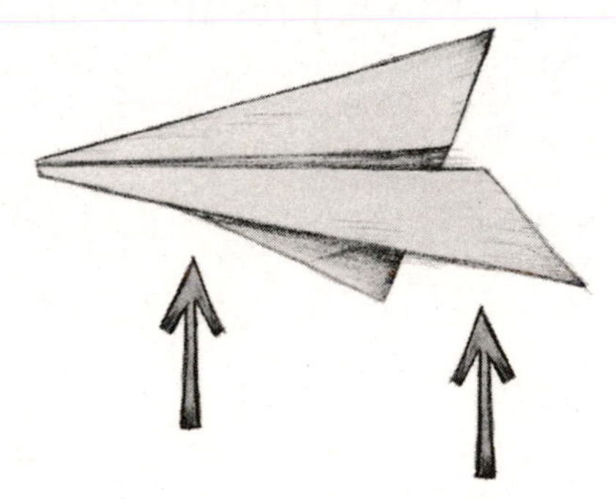

Touch the flat wings of the glider. What will the air do to the flat wings?3 Lift keeps a glider in the air.4

14

1 **Teacher Think Aloud—Questioning**

2 **Inferring**

3 **Explaining—Cause and Effect** (Push the wings up; give the glider lift.)

4 **Teacher Think Aloud—Explaining**

Lift keeps a glider in the air, but a glider also needs to go forward. Thrust moves the glider forward. A flying squirrel gets thrust by jumping from a tree. You can give your paper glider thrust by throwing it.

Your teacher will give you a pattern to make a paper glider. Do not throw your glider until your teacher tells you where you can fly it. It will need lots of room. Have fun!

How will you give your paper glider thrust? [1] What will keep your paper glider in the air? [2]

❶ **Using Vocabulary—Thrust** (By throwing it)
❷ **Using Vocabulary—Lift** (Lift; its wings)

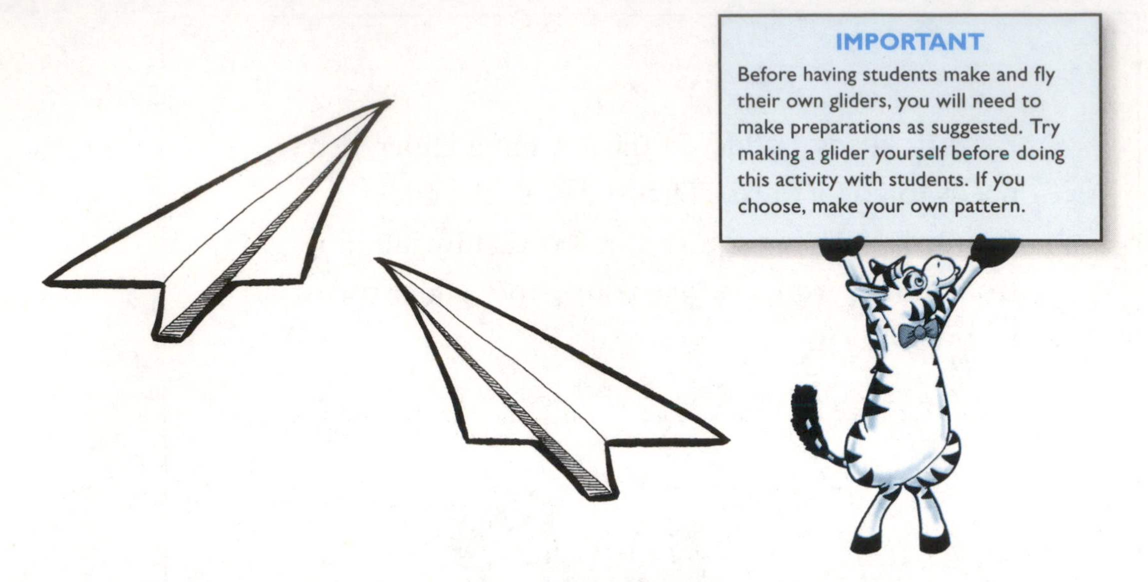

★ PROCEDURES

- Make a couple of copies of the double-sided pattern.
- Try making the glider by carefully following the numbered steps. The finished glider is sleek and fast when thrown.
- Make a copy of the pattern for each student in your group.
- Identify a time and place students can make and then fly their gliders without causing disruption.
- Have students follow the steps *with you*—one step at a time.
- Have students write their names on the gliders and, if time allows, decorate them.
- Have fun!
- To conclude the activity, remind students that air is giving the glider "lift." Then ask what is giving the gliders "thrust." (Throwing the glider gives it thrust.)

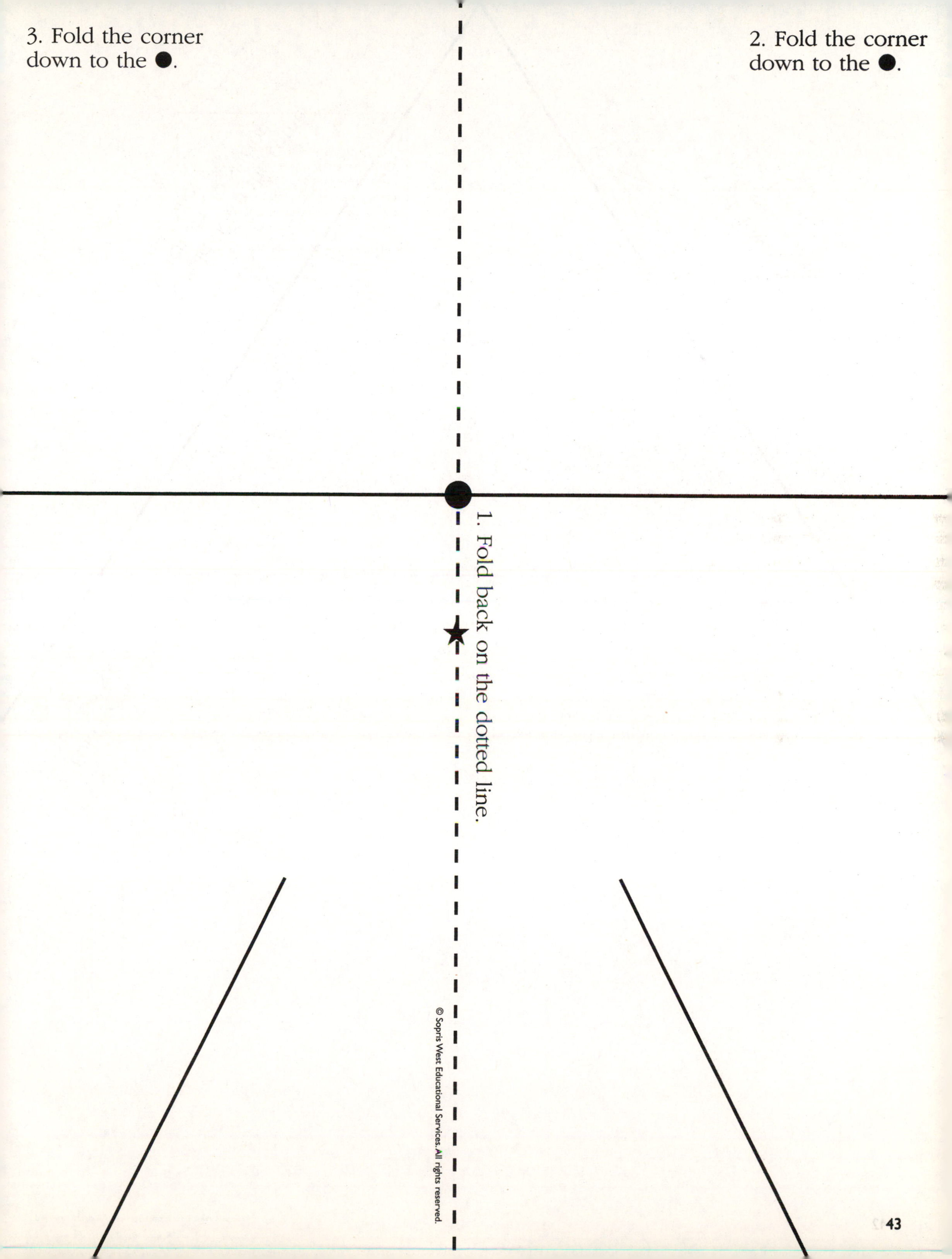
3. Fold the corner
down to the ●.
2. Fold the corner
down to the ●.
1. Fold back on the dotted line.

4. Fold down the corner.
Match star to star on
dotted line.

5. Fold down the corner.
Match star to star on
dotted line.

6. Fold to the dotted line.
Crease on solid line.

7. Fold to the dotted line.
Crease on solid line.

STORY COMPREHENSION

Use work pages from the workbook.

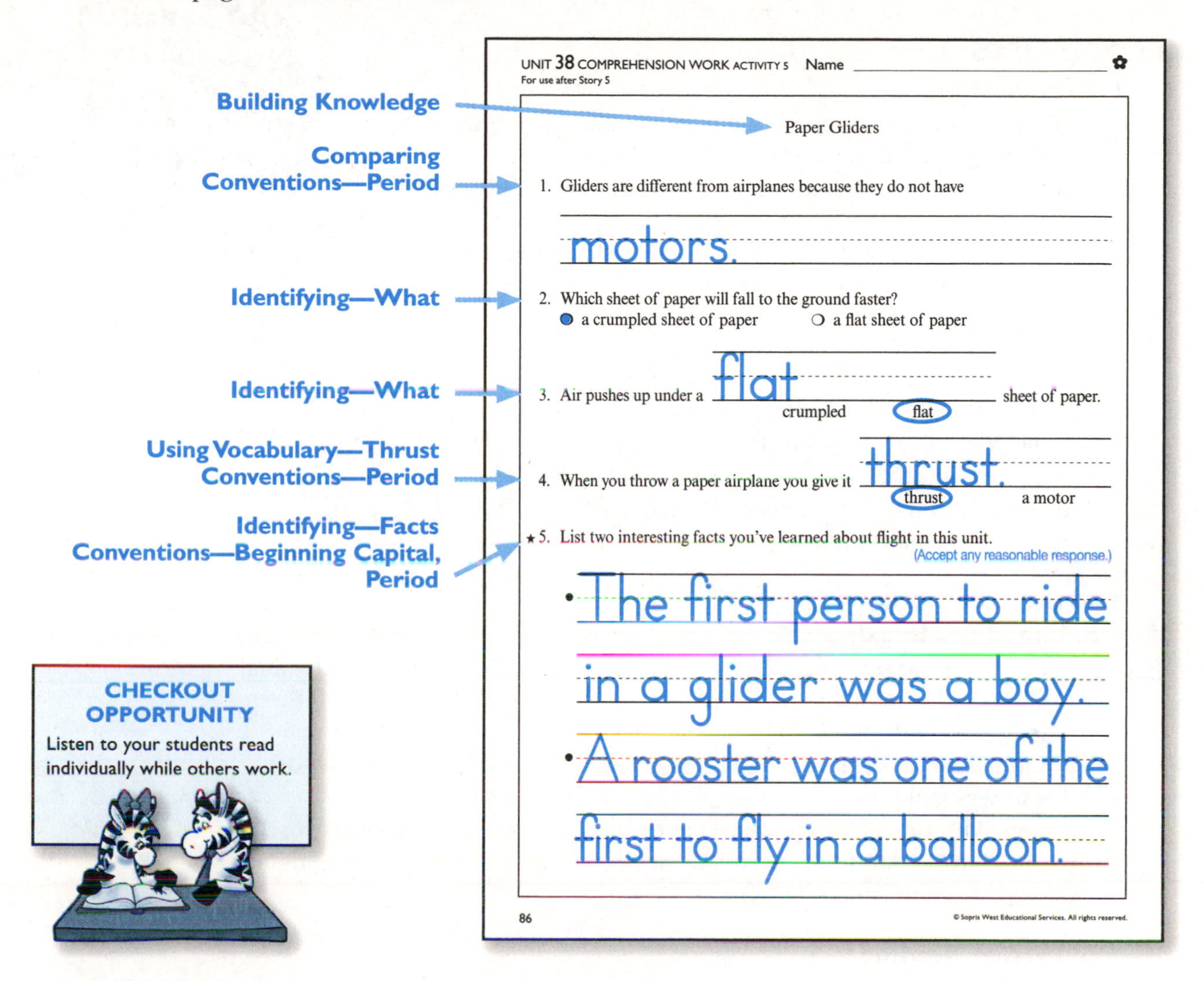

PROCEDURES

For each step, demonstrate and guide practice as needed.

1. **Sentence Completion—Basic Instructions** (Item 1)
   Have students read and complete the sentence, then end it with a period.

2. **Multiple Choice—Basic Instructions** (Item 2)
   Have students fill in the bubble for the correct answer.

3. **Multiple Choice, Sentence Completion—Basic Instructions** (Items 3, 4)
   - Have students select and circle the word that correctly completes the sentence.
   - Have them write the answer in the blank and place a period at the end as appropriate.

4. **List—Basic Instructions** (Item 5)
   - Have students read the direction and brainstorm possible responses using complete sentences.
   - Have students write two complete sentences that start with a capital letter and end with a period.

★*Note:* If needed, teach students the word "unit."

SOLO STORY READING INSTRUCTIONS

Students read from their own storybooks.

PROCEDURES

1. First Reading

- Have students individually whisper read the story, using their fingers to track text.
- After students complete the first reading and before the second reading, have students practice a paragraph. Demonstrate expressive reading for students, then give individual turns. Acknowledge student efforts.

2. Second Reading

- Mix group and individual turns, independent of your voice. Have students work toward an accuracy goal of 0–2 errors. Quietly keep track of errors made by all students in each group.
- After reading the story, practice any difficult words.
- If the group has not reached the accuracy goal, have the group reread the story, mixing group and individual turns.

3. Repeated Readings

a. Timed Readings

- Once the accuracy goal has been achieved, have individual students read the page while the other children track the text with their fingers and whisper read.

Time individuals for 30 seconds and encourage each student to work for a personal best.

- Count the number of words read correctly in 30 seconds (words read minus errors). Multiply by two to determine words correct per minute. Record student scores.

b. Partner Reading

During students' daily independent work, have them do Partner Reading.

c. Homework 4

Have students read the story at home. (A reprint of this story is available on a blackline master in *Read Well* Homework.)

STORY 6, SOLO

CHAPTER 4

Airplanes

This is our last chapter in "The History of Flight." What does the word "history" tell us?[1] In this story, you will find out about the first airplane flight.[2]

About one hundred years ago, two Americans—the Wright brothers—made the first airplane. They started by building gliders. After they learned all about gliders, the Wright brothers built model airplanes. They spent many years testing the model planes.

At last, the Wright brothers were ready to try flying in a real airplane. Their first flight lasted twelve seconds. One, two, three, four, five, six, seven, eight, nine, ten, eleven, twelve. That doesn't seem very long, does it?

What did the Wright brothers do before they made the first airplane?[3] How long did the first flight last?[4] Close your eyes. Imagine yourself in that first airplane. Now, let's count to twelve.[5] That wasn't a very long time, but how do you think the brothers felt?[6]

16

❶ **Defining Vocabulary** (This chapter is still about long ago.)

❷ **Previewing**

❸ **Identifying—What** (They made gliders.)

❹ **Identifying** (Twelve seconds)

❺ **Visualizing** (1, 2 . . .)

❻ **Inferring**

STORY 6, SOLO

Just six years after the Wright brothers' flight, a Frenchman took a plane across the English Channel. (Ask your teacher to help you look for the English Channel on a globe.) The Frenchman traveled alone, and for part of the flight he couldn't see any land.

Today airplanes are everywhere. People can travel around the world in fast jets. There are rocket ships that go to the moon. Wouldn't the Wright brothers be surprised?

Raise your hand if you've ridden in a plane. Where did you go?[1] We learned many facts about the history of flight. Let's go back to the beginning of "A History of Flight." We can look at the pictures and name the facts that we've learned.[2]

17

❶ **Making Connections**

❷ **Summarizing—Facts**

Glossary

A "glossary" is an alphabetical list of special words from a story or book. Each word is defined. This glossary has words you already know, but if you ever forget what one of the words means, you can look in the glossary. We are going to read each word, tell what it means, and then see what the glossary says. ❶

glider

A glider is an aircraft that has no motor. A glider uses the movement of air to fly.

hot air balloon

A hot air balloon is an aircraft that uses hot air and wind to fly.

jet

A jet is a fast airplane that has a powerful motor.

lift

When air pushes up on something, it has lift. An airplane's wings give it lift.

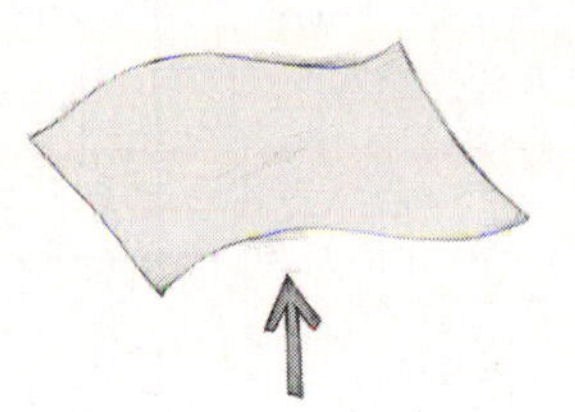

thrust

Thrust is a strong movement forward. When you throw a paper glider, you give the glider thrust.

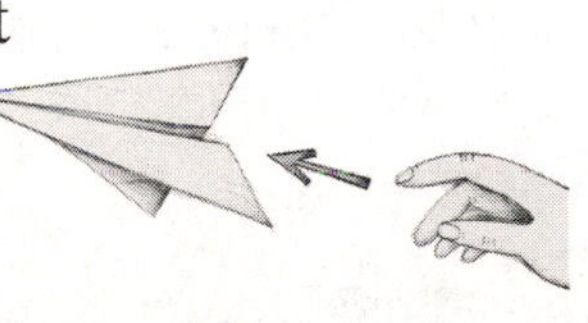

18

❶ **Defining Vocabulary—Glider, Hot Air Balloon, Jet, Lift, Thrust**

GUIDED REPORT

Use work pages from the workbook.

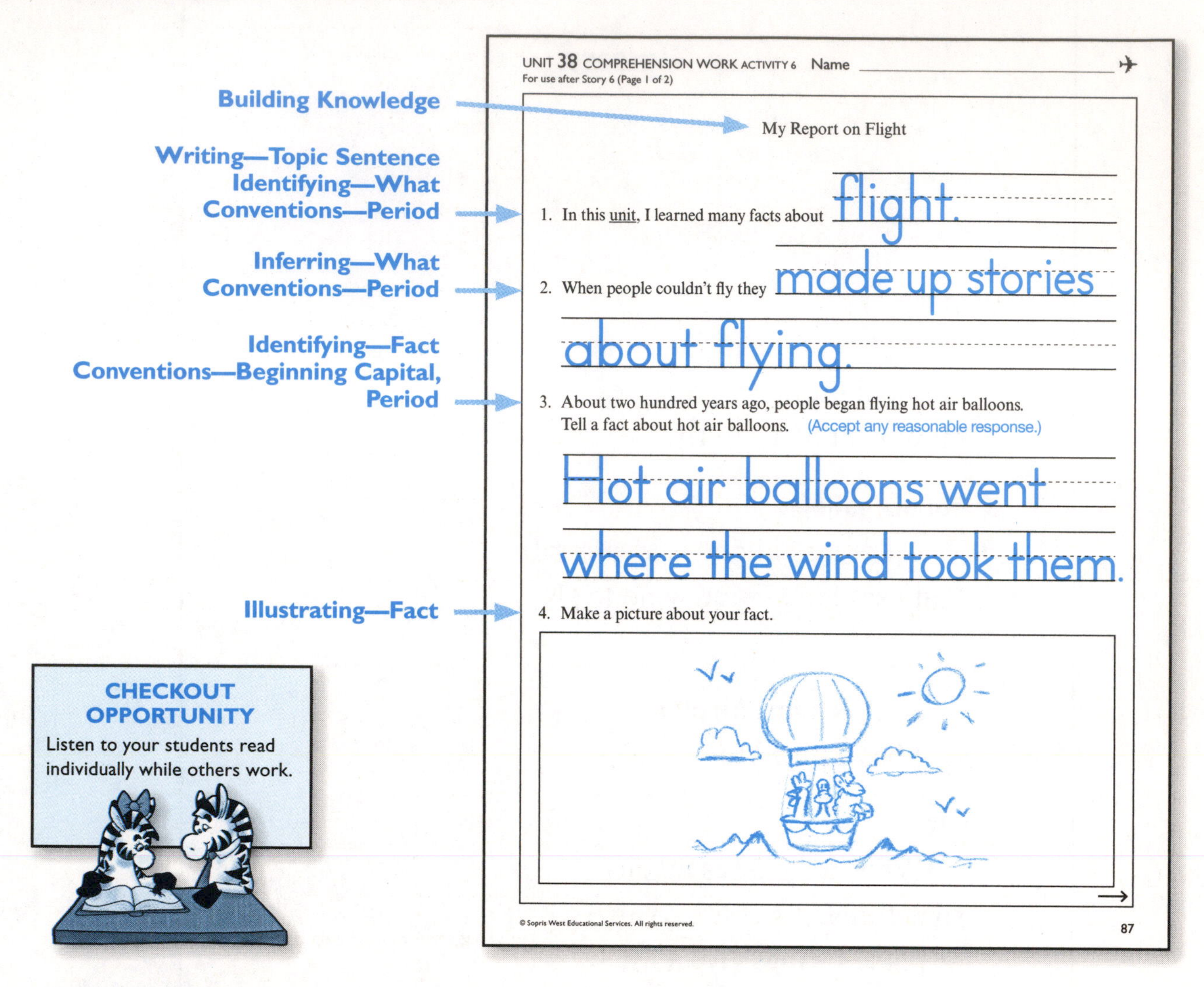
UNIT 38 COMPREHENSION WORK ACTIVITY 6 Name ____________

For use after Story 6 (Page 1 of 2)

My Report on Flight

1. In this unit, I learned many facts about flight.
2. When people couldn't fly they made up stories about flying.
3. About two hundred years ago, people began flying hot air balloons. Tell a fact about hot air balloons. (Accept any reasonable response.)

   Hot air balloons went where the wind took them.
4. Make a picture about your fact.

© Sopris West Educational Services. All rights reserved.

87

PROCEDURES

For each step, demonstrate and guide practice as needed.

1. Sentence Completion—Basic Instructions (Items 1, 2)

Have students read and complete the sentence, then end it with a period.

2. Sentence Writing—Basic Instructions (Items 3, 5, 6, 7)

- Have students read the direction and brainstorm possible responses using complete sentences.
- Have students write a complete sentence that begins with a capital and ends with a period.

3. Sentence Illustration—Basic Instructions (Item 4)

- Have students read their sentence about hot air balloons.
- Then, have them draw a picture that illustrates the fact.

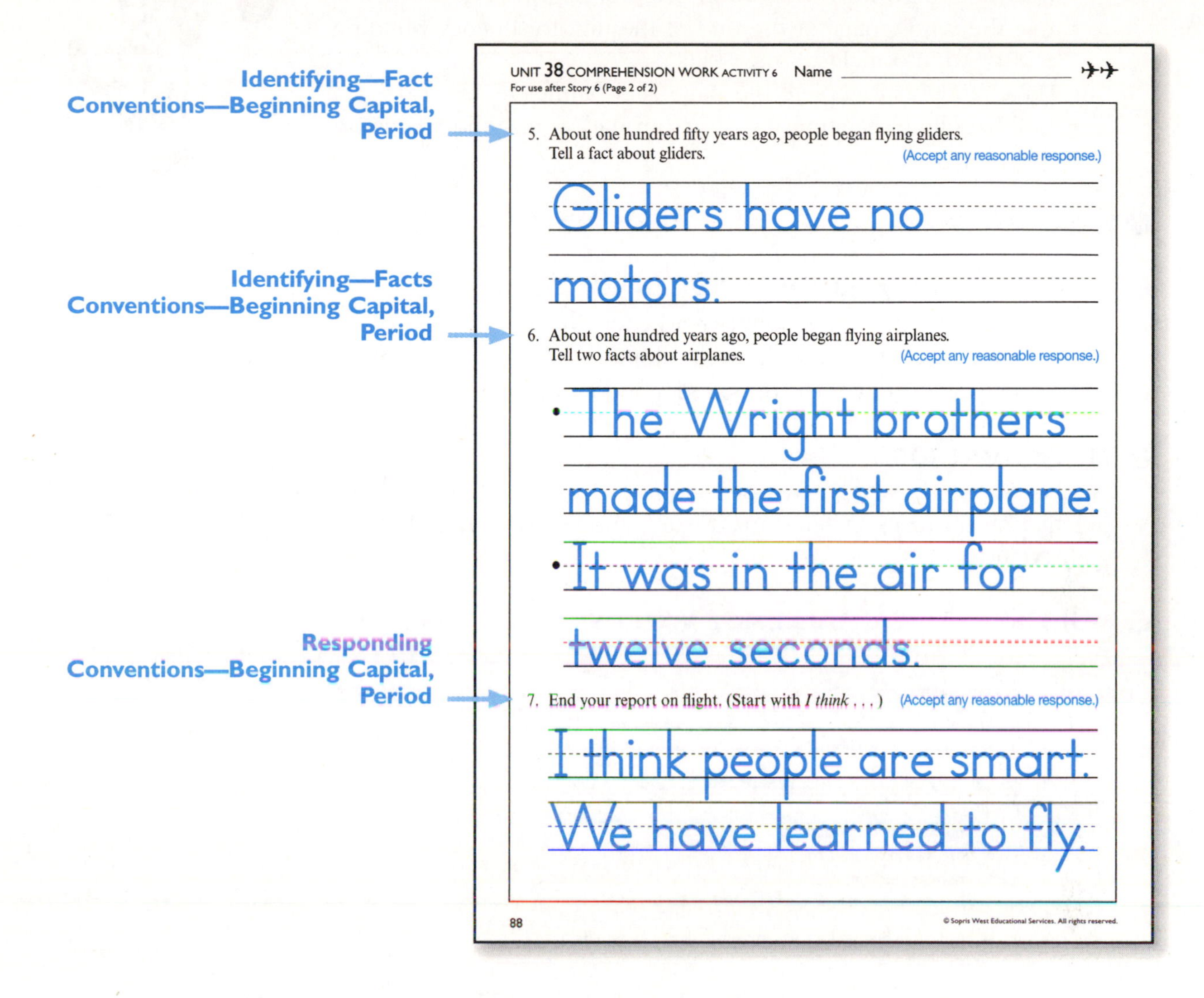

UNIT 38 COMPREHENSION WORK ACTIVITY 6 Name ______________

For use after Story 6 (Page 2 of 2)

5. About one hundred fifty years ago, people began flying gliders.
   Tell a fact about gliders. (Accept any reasonable response.)

   Gliders have no motors.

6. About one hundred years ago, people began flying airplanes.
   Tell two facts about airplanes. (Accept any reasonable response.)

   - The Wright brothers made the first airplane.
   - It was in the air for twelve seconds.

7. End your report on flight. (Start with *I think* . . .) (Accept any reasonable response.)

   I think people are smart. We have learned to fly.

88

Note: There are multiple uses for Decoding Practice 4.

- Use the Sound Review rows in place of Sound Card Practice.
- Use the whole page at the end of the unit for fluency building and/or to informally assess skills.
- Have students complete the page as a partner review.
- Build spelling dictation lessons from the sounds and words on this page.

1 SOUND REVIEW

2 ACCURACY AND FLUENCY BUILDING

- For each column, have students read each word.
- Repeat practice on each column, building accuracy first and then fluency. Mix group and individual turns, independent of your voice.

3 TRICKY WORDS

Many new Tricky Words have been introduced in the last few units. Provide plenty of practice on this section—and make sure students can read all the words fluently and with confidence.

4 MULTISYLLABIC CHALLENGE WORDS

CULMINATING ACTIVITY

Have a student roll a die and then read the number of words on the die. Have other students each cover the words with game markers.

[Jessica], you get to read two words. What's the first word in the Flower Column? (girl)
Everyone, put a marker on the word "girl."
[Jessica], what was the second word? (squirrel)
Everyone, put a marker on "squirrel."
[Jorge], your turn to roll the die.

Repeat until all students have had a turn, or until all of the words have been covered with markers.

5 DAILY STORY READING

Proceed to the Unit 38 Storybook. See Daily Lesson Planning for pacing suggestions.

UNIT 38 DECODING PRACTICE 4 ✈
(See Daily Lesson Planning for story suggestions.)

1. SOUND REVIEW Set pace. Have students read the sounds in each row.

●	igh	ch	X	ou	z	wh	-y	7
♥	Qu	ir	f	J	igh	n	ee	14

2. ACCURACY/FLUENCY BUILDING For each column, have students read each word. Next, have students practice the column.

✈	✈✈	✿	✿✿	●●
old	light	girl	air	rope
sold	night	squirrel	pair	hope
cold	right	squirt	pain	home
told	bright	chirp	rain	hose
hold	fight	bird	train	rose
fold	flight	first	chain	nose

3. TRICKY WORDS Have students silently figure out each word and then read it aloud.

☆☆	son	doesn't	put	boy	their
☆☆☆	pretty	gone	water	Only	person

4. MULTISYLLABIC CHALLENGE WORDS Have students figure out each word silently, then read the word and its definition aloud.

lightning = a flash of light in the sky; often comes with thunder
emu = a flightless bird found in Australia
Wright Brothers = American brothers who made the first flying machine

5. DAILY STORY READING
36

IMPORTANT END-OF-THE-UNIT NOTE—INCREASING FLUENCY

If students are able to read 80 words or more correct per minute, proceed to Unit 39 in *Read Well Plus*.

If students are unable to read 80 words correct per minute, go back to Unit 34 to build fluency.

End of the Unit

In this section, you will find:

Making Decisions

As you near the end of the unit, you will need to make decisions. Should you administer the Oral Reading Fluency Assessment or should you teach Extra Practice lessons?

Unit 38 Oral Reading Fluency Assessment

The Unit 38 Oral Reading Fluency Assessment is located on page 56 and can also be found in the *Assessment Manual.*

Certificate of Completion

Celebrate your children's accomplishments! When students pass the Unit 38 Oral Reading Fluency Assessment, they will have successfully completed the first grade level program.

Decoding Diagnosis

If students have difficulty passing the assessment, the Decoding Diagnosis can be used to diagnose weak skills.

Remediation

Some children may benefit from a quick recycling through previously learned skills to build automaticity and confidence.

Extra Practice

Lessons and blackline masters for added decoding practice and independent work are provided for students who need extended practice opportunities.

Making Decisions

ASSESSMENT READINESS

Assess when students are able to easily complete decoding tasks from the beginning of a lesson.

- If you aren't sure whether students are ready for the assessment, give the assessment. Do Extra Practice lessons if needed.
- If students are not ready for the assessment, proceed to Extra Practice lessons. Administer the assessment as soon as students are ready.

GENERAL ASSESSMENT GUIDELINES

- Assess all students.
- Assess each child individually.
- Score student responses on the Student Assessment Record, adhering to the scoring criteria in the *Assessment Manual.* Use a stopwatch to time how long it takes the student to read the Oral Reading Fluency Passage.
- Follow the general instructions at the bottom of each assessment. Record a Strong Pass, a Pass, a Weak Pass, or a No Pass.

ACCELERATION

- If students read with 100% accuracy and exceed the fluency goal, consider shortening units.
- If an individual student reads with greater fluency than others in his or her group, consider regrouping.

ASSESSING UNPRACTICED READING

Do not have children practice the assessments. The goal of reading instruction is to provide children with the skills to read independently. Repeated readings are an excellent tool for building fluency; however, the end-of-the-unit assessment is designed to assess how well students transfer their skills to unrehearsed passages.

INTERVENTION OPTIONS—INDIVIDUALS (WEAK PASS, NO PASS)

1. Find ways to provide a double dose of *Read Well* instruction.
   - Have the student work in his or her group *and* a lower group to review previous units.
   - Have an instructional assistant provide a Jell-Well Review.
2. Consider placement in a lower group. If one child's fluency scores are significantly lower than the other children in the group, success will be impossible without additional and intensive practice.

INTERVENTION OPTIONS—GROUP (WEAK PASS, NO PASS)

1. Extend the unit with Extra Practice lessons.
2. Consider a Jell-Well Review before moving forward. (See page 60.)

CERTIFICATE OF COMPLETION

When students pass the assessment, celebrate with the Certificate of Completion. Then, set a personal goal. (See *Getting Started.*)

CELEBRATION

You may wish to roll certificates up and present them to the students in a small group graduation ceremony.

CRITICAL ASSESSMENT

TRICKY WORD WARM-UP

does	only	water	boy	gone

ORAL READING FLUENCY PASSAGE

Take Flight Little Bird

★Chester was a little bird who did not want to fly.	11
His mother said, "Take flight, Chester. You might like it. Look at	23
your brother and sisters. They are having such fun flying high in	35
the sky."	37
Chester said, "It doesn't sound like fun to me."	46
Then one day, Chester's mother told him, "It's getting cold. We	57
must go south for the winter."	63
Chester said, "Not me. I'm staying put."	70
Soon the other birds left. When night fell, Chester was all alone.	82
Suddenly Chester shouted, "Wait for me!"	88
Chester's mother was waiting nearby. She smiled and said,	97
"That's my boy!"	100

ORAL READING FLUENCY	Start timing at the ★. Mark errors. Make a single slash in the text (/) at 60 seconds. Have student complete passage. If the student completes the passage in less than 60 seconds, have the student go back to the ★ and continue reading. Make a double slash (//) in the text at 60 seconds.
WCPM	Determine words correct per minute by subtracting errors from words read in 60 seconds.
STRONG PASS	The student scores no more than 2 errors on the first pass through the passage and reads a minimum of 100 or more words correct per minute. Place the student in *Read Well Plus* or assess for placement in a basal reading program.
PASS	The student scores no more than 2 errors on the first pass through the passage and reads 80 to 99 words correct per minute. Place the student in *Read Well Plus*.
WEAK PASS	The student scores no more than 2 errors on the first pass through the passage and reads 60 to 79 words correct per minute. Place the student in *Read Well Plus*. Provide added fluency practice.
NO PASS	The student scores 3 or more errors on the first pass through the passage and/or reads 59 or fewer words correct per minute. Provide Extra Practice lessons and retest, and/or provide a Jell-Well Review.

Certificate of Completion

This certifies that

____,

on this __________________ day of __________________, _____,

has successfully completed

Read Well 1

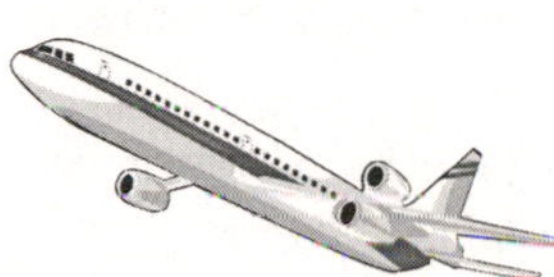

Sounds Mastered: s, e, ee, m, a, d, th, n, t, w, i, Th, h, c, r, ea, sh, k, -ck, oo, ar, wh, ĕ, -y (as in "fly"), l, o, b, all, g, f, u, -er, oo (as in "book"), y, a (schwa), p, ay, v, qu, j, x, or, z, a_e, -y (as in "baby"), i_e, ou, ow, ch, ai, igh, o_e, ir

Known Words: By Unit 37, you had learned and practiced 1,465 words.

New Words Mastered in Unit 38: Americans, boy, doesn't, England, Englishman, Englishman's, forward, laughing, only, person, push, pushes, put, son, walk, watch, watched, world, air, aircraft, airplane, airplanes, airplane's, alone, balloon, balloons, bird, birds, bright, brothers', channel, chapter, chirp, close, crumple, crumpled, dreamed, drift, drifted, drifts, drown, duck, eight, emu, experiment, feathers, felt, fight, find, fire, first, five, flap, flat, flight, flying, fold, four, French, Frenchman, fright, frightened, frightening, girl, glide, glider, gliders, glides, globe, Greeks, hail, hair, high, higher, hills, himself, history, holding, home, hope, hose, hotter, its, jets, jumping, keeps, lasted, leaps, learned, light, lightning, lighter, lit, locked, melting, might, model, motor, motors, movement, moves, night, nine, nose, pain, pair, paper, papers, pattern, plane, planes, powerful, put, rail, ready, ride, right, rocket, rode, rope, rose, sadly, save, saved, seconds, seemed, sheet, ships, smiled, softly, sold, sometimes, squirrel, squirrels, squirt, step, stretches, suddenly, surprised, teacher, testing, throw, throwing, thrust, tower, trains, traveling, twelve, wax, ways, Wright

You can now read 1,617 words—plus many other words made up of the sounds and patterns you've learned.

Note: Personal Goal Setting forms can be copied from Units 16 and 17, or from *Getting Started*.

Decoding Diagnosis

If students have difficulty passing the oral reading fluency assessment, the Decoding Diagnosis can be used to more accurately diagnose specific problems. A Decoding Diagnosis is included in the *Assessment Manual* and the Teacher's Guides for Units 19, 23, 26, 28, 30, 34, 36, and 38.

Note: If a student is unable to meet the oral reading fluency goal, he or she may have been misplaced initially, or instruction may have proceeded too fast in the earlier units. If the student makes errors related to one or two skills, you may be able to remediate these skills with intensive work. However, if the student is weak on three or more skills, he or she will need either a careful Jell-Well Review or placement in a lower group.

PROCEDURES FOR ADMINISTERING A DECODING DIAGNOSIS

1. Have the student read from the Decoding Diagnosis. Score on a separate copy.
2. For each subtest, have the student point to and read each item.
3. Make a slash through any item missed and record what the student said above the missed item.

GUIDELINES FOR REMEDIATING SPECIFIC SKILLS

Sounds

- If the student misses only one sound, continue to *Read Well Plus* but provide additional practice on the difficult sound.
- If the student makes more than one error, consider placing the student in a lower group, providing a Jell-Well Review, or systematically reintroducing one new difficult sound at a time.

Vowel Discrimination

- Have the student practice words that require vowel discrimination. Build lists of words composed of known sounds, with only the vowel changing (e.g., met, mat, meat). See the subtest examples.
- Provide additional practice on all the vowel sounds taught to date. Reteach all vowel units, while continuously reviewing all known sounds.

Beginning Quick Sounds

- Have the student practice pairs of rhyming words in which one word begins with a quick sound (e.g., went-dent, sand-hand).
- Have the student practice lists of words that begin with one quick sound (e.g., had-hid-hard).
- Reteach all units that introduce a quick sound, and review all known sounds.

Blends and Word Endings

- Have the student read lists of words that increase in length, and which include difficult blends and/or word endings (e.g., ack-nack-snack, kitt-kitten).
- Dictate words that build up (e.g., in, ink, rink, drink).

Tricky Words

- Identify the difficult words and increase practice on one difficult word at a time.
- Have the student write any difficult word and use it in a sentence.

SOUNDS

ou	P	ch	ay	j	h	ow	igh
b	qu	Y	o	v	e	d	er

VOWEL DISCRIMINATION

tap	tip	tape	top	tarp
him	harm	hem	hum	high

BEGINNING QUICK SOUNDS

best	pout	jump	girl	chick
cold	drip	her	Tom	call

BLENDS AND WORD ENDINGS

Now	chicken	gather	such	laying
market	brain	clucked	fifteen	inside

TRICKY WORDS

pretty	learn	once	head	water
only	many	their	earth	done

- Have students read from a clean copy of the Decoding Diagnosis. Record incorrect responses on another copy.
- Use information from both the Unit 38 Oral Reading Fluency Assessment and the Unit 38 Decoding Diagnosis to identify specific skill deficits.

Remediation

Prior to doing a Jell-Well Review, administer the Unit 38 Decoding Diagnosis to any student who has a Weak Pass or No Pass on the Unit 38 Oral Reading Fluency Assessment. Use the results to guide instruction as you conduct a review.

JELL-WELL REVIEW

If a student scores a No Pass, a review of earlier units is an opportunity to make the foundation of learning go from a gelatin-like substance to cement. Jell-Well Reviews enable students to gain confidence and feel successful with their reading. Go back to the last Strong Pass, and begin a Jell-Well Review. (See the *Assessment Manual* for additional information.) During the review, spend added time and practice on weak skills while quickly reviewing known skills for maintenance.

Jell-Well Planner 2

For use with Units 16–38

Planning Information Instructor ____________ Group ____________ Grade(s) ________
Last Unit Completed ______ Fluency Goal in Last Unit Completed ______wcpm
Last Unit All Students Completed With 100% or a Strong Pass ________

Assessment Results/Comments

Tentative Jell-Well Review Schedule (Make adjustments as needed.)

Jell-Well Review Unit ____ Date ________ Lesson ____	Jell-Well Review Unit ____ Date ________ Lesson ____
1. SOUND PRACTICE Sound Cards or Sound Practice, Decoding Practice 4	**1. SOUND PRACTICE** Sound Cards or Sound Practice, Decoding Practice 4
2. TRICKY WORD PRACTICE Word Cards	**2. TRICKY WORD PRACTICE** Word Cards
3. STRETCH AND SHRINK, SMOOTH AND BUMPY BLENDING Short Vowel Words	**3. STRETCH AND SHRINK, SMOOTH AND BUMPY BLENDING** Short Vowel Words
4. WORD DICTATION Dictation Examples	**4. WORD DICTATION** Dictation Examples
5. ACCURACY AND FLUENCY PRACTICE Rhyming Words Discrimination Words Multisyllabic Words	**5. ACCURACY AND FLUENCY PRACTICE** Rhyming Words Discrimination Words Multisyllabic Words
6. STORY READING	**6. STORY READING**

(See Section 5, Gimmicks and Games, of the *Assessment Manual* for ways to vary practice.)

Blackline Master 125

1 SOUND REVIEW

2 WORD DICTATION

night, each, out

The first word is "night." We're going to count the sounds in "night."
Tell me the first sound. **Hold up one finger.** (/nnn/)
Repeat with /igh/ and /t/.
How many sounds are in "night"? (Three)

Tell me the first sound. (/nnn/) Write it.
Tell me the next sound. (/igh/) Write it with the letters i-g-h.
Tell me the next sound. (/t/) Write it.
Do Smooth Blending. (/nnnight/) Read the word. (night)

Repeat with "each," and "out." Tell students the /ea/ in "each" is spelled with the letters e and a, and the /ch/ is spelled with the letters c and h. Tell students the /ou/ in "out" is spelled with the letters o and u.

CAUTION

Your children may not need Extra Practice. If in doubt, assess students and include Extra Practice only if needed.

DICTATION

- Demonstrate and guide practice as needed.
- Have students check and correct.

3 SENTENCE COMPLETION

The bird can *fly high.*

- Have students read the beginning of the sentence with you.
- Dictate the last two words, "fly high." Remind students that /-y/ in "fly" is spelled with the letter y and /igh/ in "high" is spelled with the letters i-g-h. Have students leave a finger space between each word.
- Have students trace the dotted words and complete the sentence with a period.
- Have students read the sentence.

4 ACCURACY AND FLUENCY BUILDING

Repeat practice on each column, building accuracy first and then fluency.

5 TRICKY WORDS

Repeat practice, mixing group and individual turns, independent of your voice.

6 DAILY STORY READING

1. First Reading

Have students choral read the Fluency Passage.

2. Second Reading

- Provide individual turns on sentences. Quietly keep track of errors made.
- After reading, practice any difficult words.

3. Repeated Readings

a. Timed Readings

- Have individual students read the passage while other students track the text with their fingers and whisper read. Time individuals for 30 seconds. Encourage students to work for a personal best.
- For each student, count the number of words read correctly in 30 seconds (words read minus errors). Multiply by two to determine words correct per minute. Record students' scores.

b. Partner Reading—Checkout Opportunity

While students are partner reading, listen to individuals read the passage.

Name________________________________

1. SOUND REVIEW Have students say each sound. (For -y, have students use the sound in "story.")

igh	Ch	ow	x	er	ir	Z	wh
ay	P	j	igh	or	-y	ou	g

2. WORD DICTATION Have students count the sounds in each word, identify and write each sound, and then read the words: "night," "each," and "out."

1 ____________ 2 ____________ 3 ____________

3. SENTENCE COMPLETION Have students read the beginning of the sentence. Dictate "fly high." Have students trace the words and complete the sentence with a period.

4. ACCURACY/FLUENCY BUILDING In each column, have students say any underlined part, then read each word. Next, have students read the column.

♥	♥♥	♥♥♥
each	old	night
ouch	told	light
match	cold	sight
which	fold	right
such	hold	tight

5. TRICKY WORDS For each word, have students silently figure out the word, then read it aloud.

Boy	Only	put	does	person

6. DAILY STORY READING

Name______________________________

FLUENCY PASSAGE

My Jet Flight

I was in a jet. I was going to take a flight. This was my 15
first plane flight. I felt the jet as it rose into the air. I like to 31
fly. I had been on a flight in a balloon, but never in a jet. 46
The jet was very fast. It was not like the balloon at all. The 60
balloon was not fast. 64

My personal best is _____ words correct per minute.
My goal is to read with 0–2 errors. This is what I did:

Reading	1st	2nd	3rd	4th
Errors				
Words/ 30 seconds				
wcpm				

Have students read the sentences. Time individual students for 30 seconds; mark errors. To determine words correct per minute (wcpm), count words read in 30 seconds, subtract errors, multiply times two, and record on the chart. If the student completes the passage in less than 30 seconds, have him or her return to the top and continue reading. (Repeated readings may be completed with older students, assistants, or parents.)

> **CAUTION**
> Your children may not need Extra Practice. If in doubt, assess students and include Extra Practice only if needed.

❶ SOUND REVIEW

❷ WORD DICTATION

high, girl, wait

The first word is "high." We're going to count the sounds in "high."
Tell me the first sound. **Hold up one finger.** (/h/)
Tell me the next sound. **Hold up two fingers.** (/igh/)
How many sounds are in "high"? (Two)

Tell me the first sound. (/h/) Write it.
Tell me the next sound. (/igh/) Write it with the letters i-g-h.
Do Smooth Blending. (/high/) Read the word. (high)

Repeat with "girl" and "wait." Tell students that the /ir/ in "girl" is spelled with the letters i and r. Tell students that the /ai/ in "wait" is spelled with the letters a and i.

HAVE STUDENTS CHECK AND CORRECT.

❸ SENTENCE COMPLETION

Chester is *a bird.*

- Have students read the beginning of the sentence with you.
- Dictate the last two words, "a bird." Remind students that the /ir/ in "bird" is spelled with the letters i and r. Have students leave a finger space between each word.
- Have students trace the dotted words and complete the sentence with a period.
- Have students read the sentence.

❹ ACCURACY AND FLUENCY BUILDING

Repeat practice on each column, building accuracy first and then fluency.

❺ TRICKY WORDS

Repeat practice, mixing group and individual turns, independent of your voice.

❻ DAILY STORY READING

1. First and Second Readings, Fluency Passages A and B

- Have students choral read the Fluency Passage.
- Provide individual turns on sentences. Quietly keep track of errors made.
- After reading, practice any difficult words.

2. Repeated Readings

a. Timed Readings

- Have individual students read either passage A or B while other students track the text with their fingers and whisper read. Time individuals for 30 seconds. Encourage students to work for a personal best.
- For each student, count the number of words read correctly in 30 seconds (words read minus errors). Multiply by two to determine words correct per minute. Record students' scores.

b. Partner Reading—Checkout Opportunity

While students are partner reading, listen to individuals read a passage.

UNIT 38 EXTRA PRACTICE 2 Name____________________

1. SOUND REVIEW Have students say each sound.

ou	igh	X	wh	ea	ay	ir	-y
ch	or	F	ow	j	ar	qu	ea

2. WORD DICTATION Have students count the sounds in each word, identify and write each sound, and then read the words: "high," "girl," and "wait."

1 ____________ 2 ____________ 3 ____________

3. SENTENCE COMPLETION Have students read the beginning of the sentence. Dictate "a bird." Have students trace the words and complete the sentence with a period.

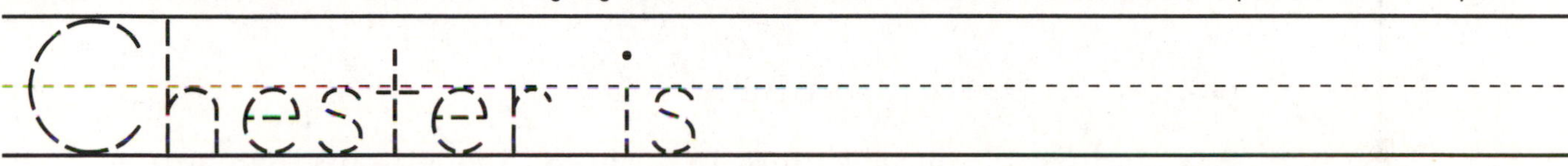

4. ACCURACY/FLUENCY BUILDING In each column, have students say any underlined part, then read each word. Next, have students read the column.

♥	♥♥	♥♥♥
close	b<u>ir</u>d	flying
nose	fl<u>igh</u>t	getting
rose	w<u>ai</u>t	staying
hose	so<u>u</u>nd	waiting
home	s<u>u</u>ch	having

5. TRICKY WORDS For each word, have students silently figure out the word, then read it aloud.

put	boy	your	brother	doesn't

6. DAILY STORY READING

Name____

FLUENCY PASSAGE A

The Flight Book

Today the teacher read us a book about flight. He 10
talked about how birds fly. He told us how they use their 22
wings to fly high into the air. It was a very good book. 35

FLUENCY PASSAGE B

We Fly

My dad took me on a flight in a plane. We rose up into 14
the air. We went up very high. I could look down and see 27
that the world was very small. "Fly higher, Dad! Fly 37
higher!" 38

My personal best is _____ words correct per minute.
My goal is to read with 0–2 errors. This is what I did:

Have students read the sentences. Time individual students for 30 seconds on one passage; mark errors. To determine words correct per minute (wcpm), count words read in 30 seconds, subtract errors, multiply times two, and record on the chart. If the student completes the passage in less than 30 seconds, have him or her return to the top and continue reading. (Repeated readings may be completed with older students, assistants, or parents.)

Reading	1st	2nd	3rd	4th
Errors				
Words/ 30 seconds				
wcpm				

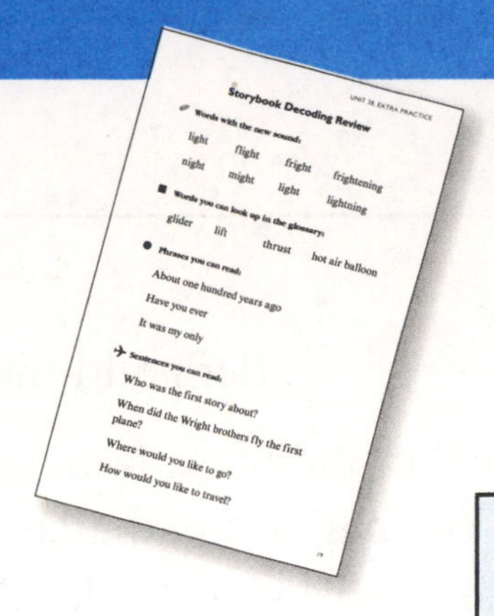
UNIT 38, EXTRA PRACTICE

Storybook Decoding Review

Words with the new sound:

light flight fright frightening

night might light lightning

Words you can look up in the glossary:

glider lift thrust hot air balloon

Phrases you can read:

About one hundred years ago

Have you ever

It was my only

Sentences you can read:

Who was the first story about?

When did the Wright brothers fly the first plane?

Where would you like to go?

How would you like to travel?

1 STORYBOOK DECODING REVIEW

For each row, mix group and individual turns, independent of your voice.

2 WORD DICTATION

Have students count the sounds in each word with their fingers, identify and write each sound, and then read the word. Use the words in sentences as needed.

day, must, shout

The first word is "day." We're going to count the sounds in "day."
Tell me the first sound. **Hold up one finger.** (/d/)
Tell me the next sound. **Hold up two fingers.** (/ay/)
How many sounds are in "day"? (Two)

Tell me the first sound. (/d/) Write it.
Tell me the next sound. (/ay/) Write it with the letters a and y.
Do Smooth Blending. (/day/) Read the word. (day)

Repeat with "must," and "shout." Tell students that the /ou/ in "shout" is spelled with the letters o and u.

> **CAUTION**
> Your children may not need Extra Practice. If in doubt, assess students and include Extra Practice only if needed.

HAVE STUDENTS CHECK AND CORRECT.

3 DAILY STORY READING

1. First Reading

Have students choral read the Fluency Passage.

2. Second Reading

- Provide individual turns on sentences. Quietly keep track of errors made by all students in the group.
- After reading, practice any difficult words.

3. Repeated Readings

a. Timed Readings

- Have individual students read the passage while other students track the text with their fingers and whisper read. Time individuals for 60 seconds. Encourage students to work for a personal best.
- For each student, count the number of words read correctly in 60 seconds (words read minus errors). Record students' scores.

b. Partner Reading—Checkout Opportunity

While students are partner reading, listen to individuals read the passage. Work on accuracy or fluency as needed.

Name_______________________________

FLUENCY PASSAGE

Beth and the Balloon

One day at the park, there was a man with a big 12
balloon. The balloon had a basket under it. The man 22
would take people up into the sky. 29

Beth was six. She always had dreams about flying. She 39
would dream about flying higher and higher in the sky. She 50
asked her father if she could ride in the big balloon with the 63
basket. 64

Beth's father told her the big balloon was called a "hot 75
air balloon." He said they could ride in the balloon. As the 87
hot air balloon lifted into the air, Beth said that flying really 99
was one of the best things. She wanted to fly forever. 110

My personal best is _____ words correct per minute.
My goal is to read with 0–2 errors. This is what I did:

Have students read the sentences. Time individual students for 60 seconds; mark errors. To determine words correct per minute (wcpm), count words read in 60 seconds, subtract errors, and record on the chart. If the student completes the passage in less than 60 seconds, have him or her return to the top and continue reading. (Repeated readings may be completed with older students, assistants, or parents.)

Reading	1st	2nd	3rd	4th
Errors				
Words/ 60 seconds				
wcpm				